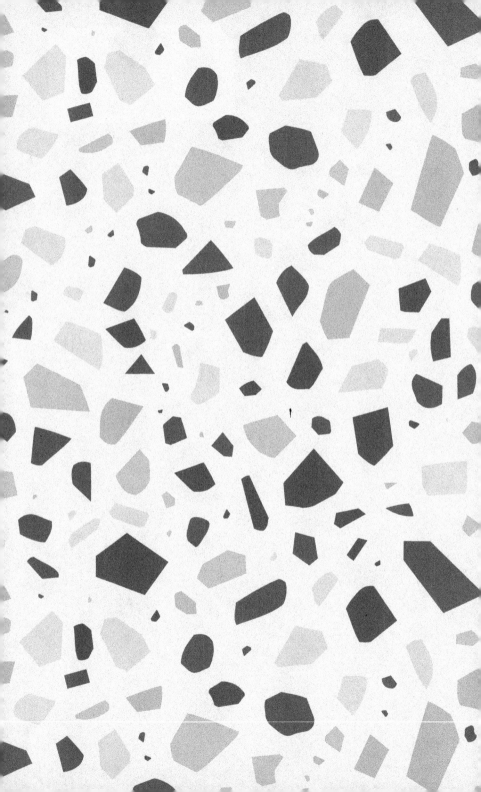

GATHER

How to Build a Mission-Driven Online Community

GATHER

How to Build a Mission-Driven Online Community

BEX BAND

A POST HILL PRESS BOOK
ISBN: 978-1-63758-640-2
ISBN (eBook): 978-1-63758-641-9

Post Hill Press
New York • Nashville
posthillpress.com

Published in the United States of America
1 2 3 4 5 6 7 8 9 10

For the Everest team that started it all:
Seanna, Becki, Nichole, Naomi, and Kate.

CONTENTS

MY ONLINE COMMUNITY

I was acutely aware of myself and my surroundings as I sat cross-legged on the double bed. The ticking from the bedside clock seemed louder than usual. I noticed I was holding my shoulders tightly, a bad habit of mine. Despite the February chill, my hands were clammy and I was feeling hot. I recognized these sensations. They are the sensations you have when you are about to do something that I call "a leap." I was standing on the edge, about to take a jump, and the drop below my feet looked huge.

Starting a Facebook group might not sound like a big deal to some, but this was one of the most terrifying moments of my life. There was little doubt in my mind about the purpose behind the group I was starting. I believed deeply in my mission to help other women kickstart a life of adventure—the same way I had. I'd recently returned from my first big adventure hiking on the Israel National Trail (INT). My body is still fresh with a tan, toned calves, and backpack chaffing marks on my hips to prove it.

This was an altogether different adventure though, one that was forcing me to face my deepest fears head-on. The public nature of an online community was magnifying my two greatest insecurities: a fear of not being liked and a fear of not being good enough. There was no escaping it. Hanging in the balance was twenty-eight years' worth of insecurities.

My finger moved across the mouse pad on my laptop until the arrow was above the "Create" button on Facebook. Was I really going to do this? I lifted my finger....

My self-doubt began from the day I stepped foot into the world. I have always been different, never quite fitting in. As a child, my tomboy haircut and thrift-shop getup (with a neck scarf to finish the look—nice!) made me stand out. Later as a teenager, while most girls were obsessing over bands, perfecting their styles, and practicing the art of cooperating with others, I was being socially awkward, opinionated, and perpetually teased. I never thrived at school. I was bad at sports, never popular, and struggled in most of my classes (largely due to having undiagnosed dyslexia for most of my school years). It was a time to be endured, not enjoyed.

The same struggles followed me when I left education behind and moved to London in an attempt to work out what I wanted to do with my life. I found myself hopping from job to job, failing to find satisfaction and my place in the world. I was on a city treadmill of long commutes, sugar-fueled snacking, and self-inflicted busyness. I lived for the weekends when I would let my hair down after a few shots, then start the cycle all over again come Monday morning. I found myself suffering from infuriating bouts of insomnia, pushing away from relationships, and spending far too much time crying.

Put simply, I was unhappy. Something had to change.

A 1,000 KM CHANGE

While on my lunch break, chewing on a Marmite sandwich, I discovered an article about long-distance hiking on the 1,000 km Israel National Trail. Instantly, I knew I wanted to do it. It would no doubt provide the change I was seeking and an opportunity to reinvent myself. I was unfit, inexperienced, and had no idea what to expect. It was a drastic decision, but it was also exciting and bold, stirring up emotions I hadn't felt in a long time.

I handed in my notice at work, sold most of my possessions, and left my rental flat. I spent the next fifty-two days (red-faced, sweating, and tripping) my way through an adventure of a lifetime, which included crossing the remote Negev Desert. I carried everything I needed in my backpack: a tent, sleeping bag, roll mat, provisions, and water. My wardrobe consisted of two outfits: my hiking clothes and what I would call my "clean" clothes. This was an outfit I would sleep and rest in which, if I'm being honest, would be considered clean by no one's standards as I'd often go weeks without having an opportunity to wash them.

Hiking the INT was the hardest thing I'd ever done. Physically and mentally, I pushed myself to put one foot in front of the other as my body battled with the relentless heat and the weight of my bag bearing down on me. But, as the weeks passed by, I felt myself get fitter and stronger and fell into a rhythm. Life on the trail was simple. I'd get up, eat, pack down the tent, walk, eat, put up the tent, and sleep (with lots of snacking in between).

This adventure brought about the change I was looking for. I felt like a different woman finishing the trail. Along the way, quite unexpectedly, I'd found a new passion. A passion to fix a cultural problem that became evident to me very early on in my journey. Of all the people I met doing the trail, not a single one had been female. Even in the courses on first aid and navigation that I'd taken to prepare, I had usually been the only woman. At times I felt I was treated differently because of my gender, even experiencing overt sexism. I noticed the outdoor groups could often be massively competitive, judgmental, and greatly lacking in diversity and inclusion.

I'd gained so much from going on an adventure. It had shaken up my life, encouraged a healthier lifestyle, and stripped back some of the stress and anxiety I'd been carrying around for years. Being in nature healed old wounds. It helped me rebuild my self-esteem and confidence while providing space for me to think clearly and creatively. It seemed like such a shame that other women weren't experiencing all this for themselves, too. I wanted women to realize how liberating outdoor adventures could be. And I wanted to be on the adventure, right there with them!

It was this desire that had me conflicted in front of my laptop, nerves coursing through my veins, my finger hovering over the mouse. I'd uploaded a photo and filled in the basic information on the Facebook group creation page, titling the group "Love Her Wild: Women's adventure community."

Would anyone join? Was I adventurous enough to run an adventure group? What made me think I was suited to lead a community? Was I about to embarrass myself publicly? Should I have more of a plan before doing this?

I paused for a moment, looking back at how far I'd come. Remembering what I'd learnt from my Israel hike about ignoring the voices of doubt and the power of taking that leap. You really never know where those brave decisions will take you.

My finger came down on the button.

Just like that, I positively changed my life and the lives of many others in ways I could never have imagined. That click of the mouse was the best thing I ever did!

GATHER

This is the book I wish I'd had with me when I clicked that "Create" button all those years ago. Building the Love Her Wild online community to what it is today has been a huge mountain to climb. Along the way, there have been many highs—passing that ten thousand member milestone, winning the first award, completing a community all-female expedition, delivering the best man speech at the wedding of two ladies who met on one of my Love Her Wild adventures—and many lows: online trolls, failed expeditions, collaborations gone sour, and the struggle to make it all financially viable.

I now stand though as the proud founder of a thriving online community that has developed into a registered non-profit—one that has been responsible for taking thousands of women on adventures all over the world. We have over thirty-five sub-communities, run by a growing team of over sixty volunteers and staff. Love Her Wild is now one of the biggest outdoor and adventure communities in the world. We have won multiple awards and received international recognition. Little old me was even named one of the UK's most inspirational entrepreneurs. I've delivered talks to rooms of hundreds, been listened to by millions on a feature for the UK's biggest radio station, and become an award-winning published author, my debut book, a memoir of my Israel hike and how that led to me launching Love Her Wild.

Really, though, that's just the flashy and visible side of running Love Her Wild. The best parts are the ones that go unseen. The acts of kindness, the forging of friendships, and the moments that change a life. I get to be the person in the middle of it all, knowing I am making a difference, even though I don't always get the luxury of witnessing it. As Charles H. Vogl wrote so beautifully in his book *The Art of Community: Seven Principles for Belonging*, "I never fully know the power of my invitations, even those that don't get responses. I simply make them because they can, and do, change lives."

It's been an incredible journey but also a very isolating and lonely one at times. Running an online community is a pretty unique job. I've often wished there were others I could turn to who "got" what I did and a manual that lessened the learning curve. It was this that spurred me to write this book.

In part, this is a practical book filled with useful advice. It will take you through the different stages of forging your community, give ideas on how to attract and maintain members, and share tips that will see you working effectively as a community leader. This book is so much more than just a how-to guide though. In times of difficulty, hearing the stories of others can be a great source of comfort and inspiration. As well as sharing my journey, the chapters ahead include interviews from community leaders from all over the world who have kindly shared their insights, challenges, and learnings to help you be the best community leader you can be.

While everyone's stories and motivations are completely different, there are some recurring themes that ran throughout all the interviews I conducted. And you should take note of these because they are important!

The first is that your community needs to be authentic and, at its heart, be in existence to genuinely help others. Your "why" for setting up the community should not simply be to make money. There is nothing wrong with monetizing your community, and I do dedicate a whole chapter on how to go about this, but this shouldn't be your main objective. A community that is built solely for the purpose of making money or launching someone's career will be missing something—the magic that makes communities so extraordinary. The glue that binds everyone together and builds trust and loyalty.

So, ask yourself: Will my community genuinely make a positive difference in the lives of its members? And do I care about making that difference in the world? Your answer to both of these should be "yes."

This leads nicely to the next common theme, which is that building an online community is hard work. Like, *really* hard work. It's likely going to drain a lot of your time and energy. There are going to be many bumps in the road ahead.

For this reason, it's of absolute vital importance that the community you build is something that excites you, is something you feel passionate about, and gets your ideas flowing. It doesn't matter if that love lies with a particular game or TV show, a sport, a belief, politics, activism, crocheting, a band, jumpsuits, stray cats, extreme ironing, a particular career, or beard art as long as you *genuinely* love it and want to spend your time talking about that topic and hanging out with people who share that same interest. You've got to enjoy it. It's the only way that you'll get through the tough patches and find the motivation to dedicate the time it's going to take to make this a success.

Finally, while you'll find a few exceptions in this book, there's also another reoccurring similarity and something that is definitely true of my own story. You don't need a sizeable trust fund or big investments to make a success of an online community. Love Her Wild was started with nothing more than a cheap, basic website and a few small admin costs. Its success relies solely on the power of your two biggest assets as an online community leader.

The first of those is social media. There has never been a better time to launch an online community. In 2017, as Facebook neared two *billion* users, Mark Zuckerberg revealed a new mission statement: "Give people the power to build community and bring the world closer together." Since then, users' community engagement is on the rise, perhaps in response to our "digital isolation" caused by increased time spent in front of screens, even more so in the wake of the COVID-19 pandemic. It is massively to your advantage that social media algorithms and users are all leaning towards groups and communities. Understanding social media and learning what works and what speaks to your people best allows you to grow and engage thousands of members (or in the case of some of the examples in this book, millions) from no more than smart posting, good engagement, and organic word of mouth without ever having to spend a penny on advertising.

Your second greatest resource is, quite simply, yourself! We are all born with a level of luck and privilege that is outside of our control. But beyond that we all have huge amounts of potential that, for most, will sadly go largely untapped. You can choose to change that and start giving yourself the opportunity to see what you are truly capable of. Increasing your self-belief and learning to be courageous takes dedication, persistence, and discipline. Spending time on bettering yourself in this way will serve your community more than anything else. Your community is ultimately a mirror of its leader. It will never be able to reach its full potential if the person driving it is bogged down with negativity, doubt, and hiding away from taking necessary bold decisions. It's for this reason that there's a whole chapter dedicated to "reaching your summit."

So now it's over to you. Perhaps you are yet to launch, or maybe you are further on in your community leader journey. Wherever you are, use this as a moment to make a decision to step up. Start believing in yourself and daring to dream big *right now*. Use the pages ahead to seek out inspiration. While it's good to learn from others and absorb advice, you should also do so selectively. Throw your own creativity and ideas into the mix. After all, you're walking your own unique path. It is your community. Your mission and your tribe of people. So, trust your instincts. Throw everything you have into making this happen and achieving your online community goals.

It might just be the best thing you ever do!

AN ONLINE COMMUNITY TO HELP OTHERS

RAMI ELGEBALI, FOUNDER OF مفقوده أطفال
(MISSING CHILDREN)

My search for successful online communities led me all the way to Egypt and Rami Elgebali. After interviewing Rami over Zoom, I leaned back in my desk chair and stared at my blank screen, trying to soak up the magnitude of Rami's online community and the immense difference it has made in the lives of those it has reached.

Was Rami one of the most inspirational people I've ever spoken to? Probably.

There was no doubt in my mind that Rami should be the first interview that I feature in this book. His dedication and flexibility led him to grow a huge community of nearly two million. His story is a strong reminder that at the core of any community needs to be a drive to do something good. To genuinely make a positive difference.

And it all began over coffee.

In 2015, Rami met with a friend in a coffee shop in Cairo near to where he lives with his wife and two children. During the conversation, his friend absentmindedly showed him a picture on his phone. A photo of a missing child who had cropped up on his newsfeed.

"This child has surely been found," Rami said, "I've seen this picture before. Probably the parents aren't aware that the photo is still being circulated."

Later that night Rami felt compelled to call the number attached to the photo to inform them that the photo was still being shared. A mother answered the phone and shared with Rami the heartbreaking circumstances of her child going missing—a boy who still had not been found many years later.

Unable to shake the story from his mind, Rami began doing more research and discovered that thousands of children go missing each year in Egypt and that, surprisingly, there is no central place for photos and information on these children to be shared publicly. He was saddened that the government in Egypt was doing very little to tackle this problem.

He immediately set up a Facebook page titled مفقود أطفال (Missing Children) and, in his own words, told the story of the boy's disappearance and the heartbreak it was bringing on his family. Within ten days the page had ten thousand followers. Within a month over a quarter of a million people wanted to help with the search for missing children. He began posting and sharing more stories—many of the parents and caretakers now contacting him directly asking for help.

Three months after launching, Rami received a photo via direct messages of someone claiming to know one of the missing children whose photo had been shared on his page. Rami's hands were shaking when he looked at the two photos side by side. There was no doubt in his mind that it was the same boy. Within a few hours, he was able to reunite the boy (who had been lost for many months) with his mother. In Rami's words, "In that moment, everything changed."

Rami had no clear plan for how Missing Children might evolve or how he might be able to better use the group to help their mission of reuniting lost children. The first step he felt was educating himself on the topic. He learned that most missing children can be found begging on the streets so, logically, thought this would be a good area to focus on. He started a campaign, asking community members to take photos of children they see begging and to send them via direct message via the Facebook page.

Using his skills as a CEO of a cybersecurity engineering company and with a group of volunteers, Rami designed and built face-recognition software. He was able to upload to the software photos that were being sent to him along with photos given by caretakers of missing children. This system was a huge success, and the number of reunited children began to increase.

The sheer volume of messages received posed a huge problem for Rami. It wasn't uncommon for him to receive one to three messages *per minute*, and each one had to be checked in case it contained valuable information about the whereabouts of a child. His wife began helping him moderate the page. Over time he brought on thirteen volunteers to monitor messages and comments, plus an additional seven to help build and maintain a website and the software.

Rami didn't stop there though. Now a couple of years since launching, Rami has managed to greatly increase his face-recognition software to include children put into shelters, as well as the deceased. After reuniting several children from shelters and hearing horrible stories of abuse, he felt it was Missing Children's duty to also find a way to protect them. Following a big push for recruitment on the community page, he brought on board over seven thousand volunteers from across Egypt who all worked in relevant professions—doctors, teachers, lawyers, and the like. With guidelines in place, their role is to monitor children in shelters and to put forward any caretakers who are suspected of wrongdoing so that they can be put on trial.

"It was this latest campaign that I realized made me a huge target," Rami told me, "There are many people behind bars because of me. I don't know who they are, but they all know I'm the guy behind Missing Children and the reason they are now in prison.

"For the first two years of running the group, I decided to stay hidden and not openly show myself as the leader of the community. But me hiding was making some suspicious, so I began to become more visible. It's given me a title and authority now which I can use to help the group. I've also noticed that the members really like knowing who I am. They want someone to relate and trust, for the page to feel more personal. My face being visible achieves that.

"One of the greatest rewards I received from being visible in my group was being chosen in 2017 as one of the top one hundred meaningful communities around the world, joining the Facebook community leadership program. From that I was able to build connections which lead to me receiving better training in safeguarding and also legal advice. A lot of press and articles came off the back of that opportunity which has all helped raise the profile of the community."

It really surprised me when I found out that Missing Children isn't a registered organization and that Rami refuses to take any money—not even donations! This surprised me in part because of the time commitment that he puts into running the community (alongside running a company full-time and being a father!). But also because of the personal strain and responsibility Missing Children puts on him. Rami has had to inform many parents that their children have sadly passed.

He holds on to the great successes in the group though as a way of staying focused. To date, he has proudly reunited over three thousand children (and now also vulnerable adults) with their loved ones.

Rami believes, "There is a difference between joy and happiness. Joy comes when you do something for yourself. Happiness comes when you do something for other people. If you want to live happy, you have to find your way to help other people. This is my way of doing that and I think God put me here to do this and make a difference via Missing Children."

Rami's three biggest community-building tips:

- Pick a good name that really represents your community well—one that clearly says what you are about.
- Try to put in place systems that make your job as easy as possible. Whether that's creating software, having rules, or recruiting volunteers to help you with the work that comes with running an online community.
- Think about how your community can really make a difference, how it can change the lives of others for the better. Remember, this is the only way you can find happiness for yourself along the way!

Find out more about Missing Children:
atfalmafkoda.com
@atfalmafkoda

CHAPTER 1

PLOT YOUR ROUTE

I was outside the cinema auditorium following a couple of bliss-ful hours of much-needed escapism. It had been a busy few weeks since I'd launched the Love Her Wild Facebook group. I hadn't expected the response to be as big as it had been. It'd been pretty overwhelming at times. First, there'd been a trickle of new members and posts in the group, but within just a few days, this had started to snowball. I had to try to stop myself from refreshing the group every five minutes—feeling a rush of excitement when another joining request popped up. My fears that no one would want to join were soon put to rest. My idea was coming to life, and women were flocking to see what my group was all about.

While I sat in the passenger seat of the car heading home, I intuitively put my hand in my pocket and turned on my phone. As the screen sprung into life, I did a double-take—my social media icons were all indicating hundreds of notifications! I opened Facebook and skimmed over the first few comments that were waiting for me.

"You OK?" my husband asked.

I just groaned in response.

It took me hours to work my way through the notifications and messages, deleting many and even making the decision to remove my first members. A fight had broken out in the Love Her Wild Facebook group, and it had turned nasty surprisingly quickly. And all because a woman had shared about a sexist comment that she'd received while out hiking.

That wasn't the only issue that had flared up. I'd made the decision to launch Love Her Wild alongside advertising my first attempt at organizing an all-female adventure (more on that later in the book). I'd posted about this adventure on Love Her Wild's public page (the group was on a privacy setting that meant only members could see any content shared in there so I also had a page for public posts) and personal profiles. These posts had been shared dozens of times, causing an explosion of activity. While the response had mostly been positive, and it had led to lots of new women joining the group, not everyone was happy with the arrival of Love Her Wild. One comment read:

"I don't know what right you think you have to open a women's only group. What's next, women-only days on the mountains? You're a sexist hypocrite. This is a joke."

Another person even messaged me directly:

"You're creating a divide in the outdoor community and it's not welcome"

Every time I read a negative comment or message (a few of them too nasty to share here), it seemed to melt away all the positive ones I'd received. They felt like a personal attack. Each one magnified, repeatedly playing on all my doubts, staying at the forefront of my mind for far too long.

When I look back on those early days of launching Love Her Wild, I picture myself looking like a rabbit in headlights. I had no idea what I was doing and no strategy for my decision-making. My actions were reactive: to new ideas that would crop up from nowhere or to responding to problems or questions that would land in my inbox.

While I sometimes look back on this fondly and have no regrets about my decisions—there's something quite brilliant about throwing yourself into something unprepared—there is no doubt that skipping some essential planning early on led to unnecessary stress and more workload. If I'd set a mission statement, it would have helped attract the right members and keep away those who weren't a good fit. Clear rules in the group from the beginning would have prevented arguments and given me something to fall back on when making decisions on removing members. As clichéd as it sounds, the author Dale Carnegie was probably right when he said, "An hour of planning can save you 10 hours of doing."

In this chapter, I'll explore all the questions you should be asking yourself before launching your community so that you can have a clear plan of action. Running a community is going to be consuming a lot of your time, so you don't want to be wasting it on things that aren't taking you in the right direction (such as spending six months building a TikTok account only to come to the realization that your target audience doesn't use this platform).

I'll be honest: I'm that person who would skip the planning chapter in a book. A bit ironic, I know, as I'm now writing one, but sometimes we don't always do what is best for us. If you are too full of enthusiasm to dedicate a lot of time to planning, I urge you to at least work out early on, what I consider to be, the three most important foundations on which to build your community:

1. Being clear (and honest with yourself) about your goals.
2. Having a solid community culture with rules to help foster this.
3. Deciding what platform is best for your community to exist on and if there are additional platforms to support this.

One final thought to keep in mind before you begin planning: although it's good to have a plan, it's important to go into the process with flexibility. Having a plan does not mean you shouldn't embrace change; roll with new opportunities; rehash and rebrand if you need to. In his book *Belong: Find Your People, Create Community, and Live a More Connected Life*, Radha Agrawal advises that "Nothing stays the same. All communities and relationships evolve and change. When you sense it happening, rather than thinking, 'This isn't what it used to be,' consider this: It's never supposed to be what 'it used to be!' Everything evolves, including communities and relationships, and it's a beautiful thing! Let's learn to embrace that!"

RUNNING A COMMUNITY AS A PARTNERSHIP

Launching a community with a co-founder (or multiple) is something that should be given some serious consideration and ground rules. If done well, it can create a beautiful team that allows you to play on each other's strengths and merge your ideas. If it doesn't go well though, it can be exhausting and a huge source of frustration. From my personal experiences, the biggest challenges that occur from partnerships are a lack of good communication, understanding between partners, and one person not pulling their weight when it comes to the workload. While I've found there are ways to improve communication and (as long as both parties are willing to have an honest conversation) resolve miscommunication, the latter can be harder to handle. On multiple occasions, I've found myself picking up the jobs of the people I'm meant to be working in partnership with and carrying out tasks that they've promised to do, even after clearly defining our responsibilities. It can be infuriating when a teammate isn't pulling their weight, and it gets even more complicated when you are meant to be splitting money or sharing titles such as co-founder. Why should the other person gain from you doing all the hard work? You can probably understand why this would be frustrating.

So before jumping into a partnership, it's important that you ask yourself *why* you are wanting to work with someone else. Some good reasons are because you want to work with someone who compliments your skills or because you aren't a natural leader and want to just focus on the admin side of the community. Some bad reasons are a lack of confidence (your confidence is going to grow in this process!) or worries about workload. If there's too much for you to do on your own, you can still bring others on board to help you. Rather than a partnership, you can assign them roles such as head-moderator or chief-blogger. This way you can build a team to support you, delegating tasks that need doing, while keeping control and freedom.

If you do decide that launching your community as a partnership is the right step for you, then think clearly about how you ensure you maintain a healthy working relationship. Regular meetings and communication (with space to address problems openly) is a good first step. Putting together a contract could help prevent confusion or problems down the line and ensure you are both working from the same place; be clear on who is doing what task.

More than anything else, you need to be going into partnerships with the right person. They need to be someone who you can be really honest with, who you can trust, and who shares your vision and passion.

The benefits of launching a community with a partner: LISA ELSWORTH AND ALEX WALKER, FOUNDERS OF BEE SOBER

Founders Lisa Elsworth and Alex Walker launched Bee Sober with the intention of normalizing and making it easy for everyone to enjoy life without alcohol. From having just one group in Manchester in 2018, they have grown to host events all over the UK. The group exists predominantly on Facebook, but alongside this, they have a telegram chat, website, podcast, and newsletter.

When I asked Alex how they encouraged that growth, she replied, "This was hard at first. We literally started off with a handful of people who had agreed to do the sober experiment (a thirty-day sober video and activities program that Alex and Lisa set up). On the back of that, we made the first Facebook group. We were in there every single day posting, sharing videos, and top tips, often just talking to ourselves.

"Bee Sober has become really popular, so whilst we still have to work really hard at promoting ourselves, being authentically and genuinely supportive every day, our love and enthusiasm for supporting our members means that a lot of our growth comes simply from recommendations and word of mouth. The members now support each other and encourage their friends to join."

Both founders see their amazing volunteer ambassadors as key to the growth of the community. Bee Sober Ambassadors can set up their own "Hives" to run socials and support in their local area. Volunteers get a wealth of benefits if they come on board, including training, discounts, rewards, and access to Bee Sober classes and workshops free of charge. Using volunteers in this way has enabled them to offer a host of in-person events that both believe are vital to keeping them all feeling more connected. The events vary from hikes, nights out, festivals, and wellness, but one thing that they encourage across all their "Hives" is a monthly brunch which happens on the last Saturday of every month.

Another factor that they see as a reason for Bee Sober's success is the fact that they were working on building the community together. As well as sharing the workload (which both Alex and Lisa have managed alongside full-time jobs), it has been an excellent example of the fun and friendship—the same fun and friendship that they hope their members can find within the community. They are leading by example. "We believe people genuinely warmed to our duo dynamic," Lisa shared. "Sobriety can be hard, and it can be a lonely place; our friendship and the events we host show that sober really doesn't have to be boring. We have fun with sobriety at the same time we like to keep it real and raw…. Everyone knows where they stand with us."

To ensure they maintain a good working relationship, they lean heavily on one of Lisa's life mottos: speak your truth. Lisa explained further, "We have both committed to doing this every day, so by being open and honest we are able to address anything and everything before problems develop. We are actually really good at this nowadays. Any problems we have had are about minor things that are left to fester, so by always speaking to each other and listening to each other without taking anything personally, we have been able to manage any potentially difficult situations."

Working together also means they can support each other through challenges. One of the biggest for Lisa and Alex was charging their members for services and membership and approaching sponsors so that they could monetize their podcast. "We really struggled at first to get our heads around the fact that we needed money to support people properly. Like most things, we supported each other to overcome these challenges. We usually find where one of us is struggling with something the other can help overcome it. Thankfully we have never had the same problem at the same time, which massively helps."

Lisa also shared some of the personal challenges she's had to overcome. "I am actually socially anxious, not ideal for somebody who organizes social events! To help me with self-confidence and anxiety, I turn to self-help books, affirmations and meditation and also used EFT (Emotional Freedom Technique). I have had to force a self-care routine, so much so, it is an in-joke of how kind I actually am to myself nowadays.

"I still get really nervous before any event. I think this helps me know how other people feel who are coming along, which means I can ensure everybody feels comfortable and safe and know the plan."

Lisa and Alex's three biggest community-building tips:

- Love what you do: it's so demanding of your heart, soul, and time that if you don't, you won't make a success of it.
- Remember your why: believe in yourself. Everyone thought we were crazy when we wanted to start a community of sober people. We could have been talked out of the idea so many times, but we kept coming back to our reason, we recognize that people who choose not to drink deserve to feel normal—and it doesn't always go right the first time. Every time we hit a bump in the road, we would just keep reminding ourselves of the people we were helping and why we were doing it; this kept us going.
- Engage: engage with your community. Even now we sometimes get so carried away with all other

admin and stuff that goes with it, we can struggle for time to engage as much as we want to. We know our members need us, and we need them. Making time to engage with your community is an absolute must.

- (And a bonus tip from Alex!) My favorite saying is that if you hang around in the barber shop too much you'll end up getting your hair cut, so make sure you choose a good barber shop; spend your time making sure you have got the right people supporting you.

Find out more about Bee Sober:
beesoberofficial.com
@beesober.cic

BE A SPONGE

While I made a lot of mistakes early on, the one thing I did right was absorb anything and everything I could from others. I began by carrying out lots of research: joining dozens of other groups, reading biographies and blogs written by community leaders, consuming podcasts and YouTube talks, and getting to know the key players in that space from public figures to big-name brands. I examined what the successful groups were doing that seemed to be working well and noted things I saw that I didn't like. Within a few months, I had a really good feel for the industry I was working in (outdoor and adventure) and could tell you what events were happening, who were the biggest target audiences, and who the important people were to know.

I approached my new venture with a thirst for knowledge. Right from the beginning, I could see that the individuals who were making the biggest success from running online communities seemed to be really savvy and have lots of useful skills under their belt. There was a lot to learn that could help me, from social media marketing to pitching to sponsors. We are so lucky to live in a time where there are endless amounts of free resources to be found online via blogs and YouTube tutorials and in all the business books you can find in your nearest library. I'm constantly absorbing knowledge from these resources—even today—and if there's ever a talk or a business event happening nearby, I'm there taking notes.

Looking back on my journey, I can see how this "sponge" mentality has served me so well. Those knowledge and skills have been invaluable. In the well-known business book *Rich Dad Poor Dad*, author Robert T. Kiyosaki says, "I am concerned that too many people are focused too much on money and not on their greatest wealth, which is their education. If people are prepared to be flexible, keep an open mind and learn, they will grow richer and richer through the changes. If they think money will solve the problems, I am afraid those people will have a rough ride. Intelligence solves problems and produces money. Money without financial intelligence is money soon gone."

WHAT ARE YOUR MAIN GOALS?

You are going to be the driving force of your online community, so it's worth spending some time understanding what your motivations and goals are for setting one up. This will greatly influence the decisions you might make along the way. It will also be something you can come back to in tricky times to remind yourself why you are doing this in the first place.

You will likely have more than one goal, but try to establish which are the most important to you (I suggest one or two) followed by secondary goals (two to three). Set aside some time to really think about this and try to be honest with yourself (for example, let go of any guilt you might have about making money or feelings that it's somehow a negative thing to want to be known as an authority in your field).

Here are some ideas of the sort of goals you might have for your online community…

- Make a positive difference in the lives of others in X way.
- Build a career for myself doing something I love.
- Gather like-minded individuals.
- Make new friends.
- Tackle a social or ethical issue.
- Have more flexibility with my work days.
- Be the go-to spokesperson in my field.
- Run a successful annual event.
- Make enough money to afford X.

NAIL YOUR NICHE AND TARGET AUDIENCE

You can't be a community for everyone! The beauty of a community is that you are bringing together individuals who have a very specific shared or common interest.

It can feel like having a really small niche is preventing you from growing or alienating too many people, but the opposite is true. It is well known in the business world that the more of a niche you have, the easier it is to grow. That's simply because your brand will be easier to define and will speak to its intended audience. Having a specific and clear label also feeds a sense of identity and belonging, which is exactly how you want your members to feel.

Furthermore, you are going to need to have a good sense of your members and who your community is for. This is called your target audience. Understanding your target audience will allow you to carry out research so that you can understand their behavior, where best to find them, and how to communicate with them.

You can really lean into this by having two niches, so you are a community for X and Y. For example, you might want to set up a freediving community for your area. Initially you think "I'm a community for everyone because anyone can like freediving." But then you discover there's already a group similar to yours in existence. On closer inspection though you see that this particular group is heavily geared towards freediving spearfishing. These are not your people! You wanted a group for free divers who are more interested in conservation and simply observing wildlife while practicing the sport. Your groups may be for the same sport, but their personality and target audience are going to be very different. You can now be clear on your target audience—free divers from my area who are passionate about protecting marine life and, in time and following some research, you realize this style of freediving mostly attracts young people aged twenty-five to thirty-five. Now you've got all the information you need to deliver a well-defined community with a clear purpose and know exactly how best to reach your intended audience.

This works no matter what your topic. So rather than simply being a chess club, could you be a chess club for LGBTQ+

players? Rather than being an air-soft enthusiast group, are you an air-soft enthusiast group for New Yorkers?

WHAT DOES YOUR BRAND LOOK AND FEEL LIKE?

This might feel a bit strange to think about, but your community will be a brand. It'll have a name and a look. Something that will (hopefully) be instantly recognizable to your members and perhaps even further afield. You'll save yourself a lot of hassle if you can get your brand looking and sounding good from the start.

Below I've listed the different areas of branding that you are going to have to consider. The key is consistency. Across all your platforms you want the logo, visuals, and wording to be the same. The tighter your branding the more professional and trusted you will appear, and the quicker you'll become a recognizable community.

1. Decide on a name

Choosing a name can be a daunting task. I often get asked how I came up with the name Love Her Wild. Quite simply, I went onto a website domain platform and tried a huge number of different combinations of relatable words until I found something that hadn't been taken—loveherwild.com. It wasn't well thought out, but the name has served the community well over time. It's short and memorable. It speaks to our audience of "Her" and suggests what we are about—connecting women to the "Wild."

If you are struggling to come up with a name, ask friends and loved ones for ideas and suggestions. Use a thesaurus to find similar words to your community's interests and purpose. Once you've got some ideas, check that they aren't already being used.

As soon as you've settled on a name buy the domain name (website address) and set up an account on all social media platforms; even the ones you aren't intending to use (you never know if this will change down the line, plus this will prevent any unfortunate copycats).

2. Define your mission

Have a snappy, one-line statement that clearly says what your community's purpose is—and even better if you can make this a tagline. It's helpful to have this from the start as you can use this as your description on social media profiles and website if you choose to have one.

3. Establish your ethos

This is an important step and will help you shape the tone of your community as well as help you stand out from others in existence. One of the reasons I set up Love Her Wild was because I didn't like the competitiveness and judgments I received when joining other outdoor clubs and groups, where I was often the only woman. I wanted to create something different. A space that was supportive and kind. So, I used this to define my community ethos: "we always put kindness and teamwork before achieving any adventure goal." This culture has helped us stand out from other, more competitive women adventure groups.

Ask yourself, what is important in your community? What attitudes do you want your group members to embrace?

Once you've settled on your ethos, you then need to work out how you will translate this to members. Perhaps the easiest way is simply having "rules" for your community that new members need to agree to follow upon joining (keep them short and lighthearted; you don't want to put people off by having too many). Most social media platforms that support communities will have this as a feature. On Facebook, for example, you can set it so that all new members joining your group need to agree to follow the rules before being approved.

Having rules is not only great for translating your ethos but will also help prevent disagreements in the group. They will be your backup should the time come that you need to remove someone from the group (for example, if someone is leaving offensive comments).

There are other ways you might choose to set the tone of your community. We have scheduled posts to encourage kindness and sharing in the group and reminders that any meet-up always starts with a brief introduction from the organizer, who emphasizes that we are a team and are there to look out for each other. Small actions like this can have a big effect on group behavior.

A note on promotion: your community grows, it will become a valuable resource for other companies and brands who will want to target your tribe of people. Your group will likely become filled with adverts to buy this, join this, support this! These will greatly impact your ethos and efforts, so protect your community space from the start by including a no-promotion rule. If you want to allow members an opportunity to self-promote, this is best done in the form of a weekly or monthly dedicated post or discussion where promotion is kept to the comments only.

4. Brand yourself visually

Creating consistency visually is the easiest way to make your community instantly recognizable Ask yourself:

- What will your logo be?
- Fiverr.com is a great website for finding affordable designers, or you can create your own on canva.com using one of their free templates. If you already have a decent number of members, perhaps you could create a competition for community members to come up with a design, or a poll could decide the winning logo.
- What will your color scheme be?
- Pick two to four colors to be your color scheme. Stick to these chosen colors as much as possible if building a website, choosing social media coloring schemes, or creating posts with images and text.
- What photos will represent your community?
- Having a handful of photos that represent your community and what it stands for will prove really valuable as you grow. You can use this for your cover photos, when needing a generic photo for a post, or to pass on to interviewers and journalists if you get any media attention. You can use a free photo stock website (like unsplash.com)—although it's much better to get authentic photos from your community if you can.
- Will you have merchandise?
- Merchandise can make members feel a part of something and can be used to foster exclusivity, something that can encourage a sense of belonging. Websites like teemill.com make it really easy to create merchandise; for example, T-shirts that your members can buy with the community logo on them. If you do meet-ups, always encourage members to wear their merchandise.

Along with available T-shirts and sweaters, I created a series of patches that members can buy to sew onto their hiking bags or beanies. They have a real "boy/girl scout" feel, and members love them! This led to me creating an exclusive patch that only our volunteers get. You could also create a membership card like the one members get when joining the H.O.G club (Harley Owners Group) which gets them into meet-ups, the Harley-Davidson Museum, as well as discounts with partnering brands.

5. Create a language

Decide what language your community will use. Having inside jokes, catchphrases, nicknames, and titles will all help cultivate a sense of community.

As a bare minimum, you should choose a name for your members, ideally something that will make them feel special. The Canadian-born singer Justin Bieber cleverly coined a name for his fans: "Beliebers." His fans began using the term, creating fan pages on forums and social media to share their love for the singer. I choose to refer to members of the Love Her Wild community as Wilders—a term that came organically from within the group as members were sharing posts.

You also need to decide what you will call your community. Decide whether it is a community, group, tribe, family, fans, and so on.

Fostering your brands community and culture: WES BOWIE, ORIGINAL MEMBER OF SOLO ARMADA

The story of how the Solo Armada community was formed is shared in detail on their website. It begins: "It's 12th May 2017 and it's the first day of Frank Turner's Lost Evenings weekend: a series of four nights at the Camden Roundhouse for Frank to do what he does best. Thousands are travelling to the capital not just from the UK but from around the globe. However, for some the journey was not of excitement but of nerves, apprehension and a sense of the unknown. These people travelled alone to an event where they knew no one, because no matter what, they HAD to be there."

Via social media networks, individuals heading to the gig alone arranged to meet in a nearby pub, "Speak to any of the people that travelled alone that day and they will find it hard to put into words what happened. Over the next days a Facebook message group formed so we could arrange where and when we were meeting and who was doing what. Matching tattoos were discussed (which some did indeed following up with!).... These people have become friends through a mutual love of music. These people are already planning when they are going to see each next and at which gig. These people have become the Solo Armada."

Solo Armada was formed accidentally, spurred by Wes and a number of other "Originals." There was no plan, and the group has grown from pre-gig meet-ups to a website, articles, and even putting on their own gigs. Facebook has been integral to the community forming and growing. As Wes explained, "Having a Facebook group allows so many more people to contribute with content/posts, etc., so that it's not just down to one person or admins. Having it private and so that people have to request to join also helps keep the spammers away. We have a series of questions you have to answer to join." Solo Armada has three clear rules:

1. Support music!
2. Enjoy yourself!
3. Be more kind! (*Be More Kind* is an album by Frank Turner).

Solo Armada are a great example of how branding, language, and merchandise can be used to strengthen bonds within a community. One thing they introduced are badges; each year they produce a new design in a set number, so once they're gone, they're gone. Wes told me more about their success, "The main thing with the badges…they get people talking. They get them communicating and they start conversations. This was never the intention but it's what we've noticed. For me when I'm at a gig on my own, which I still get anxious about, if I've got my badge I feel like I've got my gigs mates there with me as cheesy as that sounds. It feels like someone has your back."

Wes's three biggest community-building tips:

- Be a *PART* of the community! Why did you start it in the first place?!
- Don't be rigid with how you think the community should be or your expectations. It's called "community" for a reason because it's a naturally evolving place, and you have very little control over that.
- Have fun with it, be yourself, and, most importantly, don't take yourself too seriously.

Find out more about Solo Armada:
soloarmada.com
@TheSoloArmada

SET COMMUNITY RITUALS AND TRADITIONS

Richard Millington, the founder of the community consultancy FeverBee, said in a blog on his website, "Every community would benefit from having a ritual that newcomers go through. Avoid the shocking and go for something fun and interesting. Try to get members emotionally invested in the community."

We've all heard of sports teams or school societies that have quirky traditions or rituals that all members must undertake. While it might initially seem a bit silly, it could serve a great purpose. It engages new members and instantly creates a shared experience that members can connect over.

For Love Her Wild, I started an "open mic" tradition at our events where members are encouraged to stand up for a few minutes and share a personal story, a goal, read a poem, or teach a skill. It doesn't matter what the content is—it's the standing up and sharing that makes them feel like a bigger part of the event and community. I enhanced this even further by renaming this ritual "Wild Words" (adding to our group's exclusive vocabulary).

Can you think of some traditions that might bring your community together? They don't all have to be so bold. Millington uses a great example in the same blog post of the CMX Summit: a tradition of getting everyone on their feet clapping as speakers walk onto a stage. He explains, "It's fun for participants and a buzz for speakers."

I can't think of a better example of cultivating community through rituals than Tough Mudder. Tough Mudder is an endurance obstacle race founded in 2010 in America. By 2016, more than three million people worldwide participated in a Tough Mudder race. What makes Tough Mudder stand out from other races is its sense of community and the fact that it isn't a race at all. There are no timed entries, no winners, and many of the obstacles require teamwork.

In his business autobiography, *It Takes a Tribe: Building the Tough Mudder Movement*, co-founder Will Dean talks a lot about cultivating a culture in his HQ team and this filtering down to participants of the Tough Mudder. From the beginning, they were determined to do their own thing and create their own rules.

Before each race, participants (known as Tough Mudders) gather around an MC who reads out a heart-pumping inspirational manifesto which all "Mudders" must shout back aloud together. Words like "no one is better than your best, but your best will make you better" blare before participants before setting off following a klaxon, running through smoke grenades. On completion of the course, Tough Mudders are awarded a bright, instantly-recognizable headband. As part of their "Tough Mudder Legion" program, repeat participants receive different colored headbands, so they visually stand out as loyal members at races. Tough Mudder celebrated its first "100 Legionnaire" with a handcrafted steel headband.

WHAT PLATFORM WILL BE THE HUB OF YOUR COMMUNITY?

You are going to need to decide what platform will be the hub of your community. A space where members can ask questions, converse, and you can make announcements and share content and/or posts. Ultimately, a place where your members will form and maintain relationships.

There are three different ways to approach this. While you could use more than one, I advise against this as it is time-consuming and will fracture your members' engagement. Keep things simple and focus on building one space effectively rather than spreading yourself too thinly.

1. Build and host your own platform

Building your own platform could take the form of a website where you install a space where members can communicate. Mumsnet and Money Saving Expert are examples of communities that have done this. Their websites are a wealth of knowledge and content, but at their heart are active forums, organized into different topics. Members need to create a log-in to access and interact on the forum.

Don't feel like you are limited to simply forums though, as there might be a different structure that works better for you. The Naturally Curly online community has created a "Style Nook" section on their website where members (who all have curly hair in common) can share and browse styles for inspiration. An alternative could also be to build an app. Michelle Kennedy set up the Peanut App community after the birth of her first child. She had so many questions and worries but felt like the online forum spaces available weren't suitable for providing her the support she needed. The Peanut App connects women in their area who are going through similar life-changing stages—puberty, pregnancy, or menopause—via members' profiles, discussions, and direct messaging. The platform works similar to a dating app (minus the swiping!) and hosts over 1.5 million women from the UK, the US, and Canada.

Hosting your own platform gives you complete control and flexibility. You can choose your interface, branding, and add extra features such as events pages or galleries. This freedom will also help you if you plan to monetize. You could set up a shop, for example, or add advertisements as and where you like.

The yoga sensation Adriene Mishler has built a successful community, deciding to set up both a website forum and an app (where members pay a monthly subscription to get access to exclusive yoga lessons and classes). It's important to note that Adriene began on YouTube, putting out her content free of charge, and growing a following to over four million.

One of the biggest considerations, if choosing to host a community in this way, is that members have to actively visit your site or download your specific app. This provides an altogether different challenge if you aren't starting out with a huge multi-million following. It's hard to get people to register for something new—it's not impossible, but it takes a bit more convincing than something that is a simple click on a familiar preexisting platform.

There are other considerations: building the platform could take a lot more time and money. Alongside that, there will no doubt be a lot of updates and technical glitches as it grows.

Growing an online community on an online forum: ELIZABETH BENTLEY, FOUNDER OF SCHOOL LIBRARIANS' NETWORK (SLN)

Elizabeth Bentley's online community came off the back of a master's. In her own words, "I was studying for a Master's in Education, designed specifically for school librarians. I planned to write my dissertation on the professional isolation of school librarians and how it could be combatted. As part of my research, I created SLN to see what difference it might make. It was based on the much bigger LM_NET in the States which was started in 1992 by university professors, and is therefore hosted on a university server. I was not able to host it on JISC, which only hosts higher education lists, which is why I used Yahoo Groups initially.

"Twenty-five years ago, social media, apart from email and online forums, was much less developed, so spreading the word was very slow initially. I was able to put a small announcement in librarians' professional journal. I also handed out flyers at professional development events. It took about four months to start to grow, but then it grew largely by word of mouth.

"I never got round to doing the dissertation, so I never got the master's, but I always feel SLN has had more impact than any dissertation."

Members' replies to discussions are sent directly via email, and they can also view the forums online. While the downside of members receiving emails is that they can get overwhelmed if there are a lot of replies, it does mean that members are kept highly engaged.

When I asked Elizabeth what her biggest challenges were managing the group, she said there were three:

"Confidentiality: We have had a few incidents where emails have been shared outside the list, and members have been threatened with disciplinary action or similar. We now ask all members to agree to our confidentiality. But there is no real way of policing it, so it is all on trust.

"Moderation: When I started SLN, I somewhat naively thought that school librarians were all such nice people that moderation was unnecessary. While this is largely true, we have had occasional problems. This is partly due to the nature of emails (indeed, and online communication), and we are probably more used to it now, but I know it is still an issue. What may seem like acceptable phraseology may be experienced quite differently by the recipient or others.

"And time: I try and read all messages, and in the early days I responded to as many as possible where I felt I could help. I also have to respond to all requests to join to check ID and get the confidentiality agreement. While I was still working, I read SLN emails in the evening, as

I never had time at work, though I know some librarians manage it. So, it was all on top of a full working day!"

Elizabeth's three biggest community-building tips:

- Patience in the early stages.
- Being responsive to issues as they arise, good and bad.
- Having a genuine reason for people to be part of the community and take an active interest.

Find out more about SLN:
groups.io/g/SLN

2. Community-specific platforms

If you don't want the effort of building your own platform from scratch, you could choose a third-party platform. There are many that have been built specifically to cater for online communities. They include Reddit, Meetup, Tribe, Circle, Hivebrite, Mighty Networks, and GroupApp. There are many more available depending on the sort of features you'd like to have. Most of these effectively act as a white-label software where you can build and customize (to some extent) a community. It will save you time and money having to build your own platform, and they are relatively easy to use, as there are many coming with support centers to assist you with setting up.

The benefits of using these community-specific platforms are that they are usually free of charge or low cost, easy to use, and somewhat familiar to users—although for many of your members, you are still going to need to convince them to set up a new log-in or download an additional app.

The downside is that you don't have the same ownership than if you hosted your own platform. You are not going to have the same level of freedom when it comes to monetizing and creating interface options.

Growing a community on Slack:
FRAZER RILEY, FOUNDER OF QUEER SURF CLUB

Frazer Riley started the Queer Surf Club in the midst of the COVID-19 pandemic, so existing in a digital space was necessary. The community exists to foster a sense of belonging and commutation amongst queer surfers— something that is especially important as extreme sports traditionally overlook or exclude the queer community.

This global community is hosted predominant on Slack. Frazer explains his reason for settling on this communication platform: "Slack enables our global community to connect and self-organize. With the right set up, parameters and community agreements—it enables us to grow QSC organically, whilst fostering a sense of community belonging."

He highlights some of the best features (which are all available on the free version) including:

- The ability to create different channels as well as manage all of their events and meet-ups.
- The reactions feature which allow members to react to each other's messages and allows them to

do votes, gather information, and plan ahead for events. (One example is, whoever needs surf hire for a meetup can react with a surfer emoji.)

- Helpful bots, such as GreetBot, which sends all new members an automated message of what they need to do when they join have made growing a community easier.

Along with launching a community in a global pandemic, Frazer has had to overcome several other challenges. A lot of them ring true for many of the community leaders interviewed in this book such as perfectionism, Imposter syndrome ("It feels weird to be centering yourself so much in it."), and setting boundaries both personally and within the community. Frazer expands on the latter:

"Growing a community can feel like never ending, there's always something else that can or should be done (and your community will be the first to tell you this…), not losing yourself in this and getting overwhelmed is key (building communities is a long game).

"Managing communities means you're constantly juggling a flux of folks joining, folks leaving but also the occasional drama or ruler breaker. For the sake of the community, boundaries need to be defined on what is, or isn't acceptable, and sometimes people need to be removed. Being OK with having direct and difficult conversations with members (and keeping the best interest of the community at the core) is key."

Despite the challenges, Frazer has done an incredible job of fostering a sense of belonging in his community in a relatively short space of time. "One of the main things that has created this is, by really focusing on our niche (queer and ocean-lovers) and centering our entire organization, brand and values round this. Secondly, by constantly asking for feedback, adjusting and giving our community members to create (their own mini meet ups, channels, artwork, zines, and more).

"From this, this is where the success of QSC grows. Our community members are our biggest advocates and they continuously tell their own networks about it. Whether that's online, or offline. Our community continues to grow organically that way."

Frazer's three biggest community-building tips:

- Focus on your niche (and the solution): communities that thrive have shared commonalities. In particular, those with a really focused niche have a specific shared interest. Dig into what your niche could be and center it at everything you do. Being both queer and a surfer or ocean-lover is pretty niche, but if we were broader than this, we'd miss key commonalities that bound us together. Secondly, by creating this niche, what are you going to solve for the community? For us, we pride ourselves on being a place for queer folks with common interests to connect and to enjoy nature (the ocean) together. Again, we center this with our brand and at our meetups.

- Aim for self-organization: when you first build a community, it's going to take up a lot of your time and resources. You quickly learn to become a jack of all trades, while constantly being on in building your community. Whatever platform you use, your community needs a reason to come back—that can be as little as you providing input, starting conversations, or sharing updates. That, however, is not sustainable. There comes a tipping point in communities where success depends on self-organization. Give your community the right parameters to self-organize in, to run with your community, and create on their own. You can reinvest your resources into other areas of community management while watching your community self-organize and grow organically.

- Listen and innovate: your community is going to talk if they don't like something, so create an environment where it's easy for them to share it with you. Creating upstream feedback is key for community growth, to ensure your community members feel they have a voice, and their opinion matters. We collect feedback after every meetup, have a dedicated Slack channel for it, and ask folks in person. This enables us to constantly innovate and evolve the QSC community.

Avoiding this can create resentment or a sense of unimpressionable hierarchy, both of which are detrimental to fostering community.

Find out more about Queer Surf Club:
queersurfclub.com
@queersurfclub

3. Social media platform

Most online communities opt for the third and final option: launching on an existing social media platform. Billions of people use social media every single day, the most common include Twitter, Instagram, WhatsApp, and YouTube. Because of their ability to reach audiences beyond your network and their group features, there are two platforms leading in the online community space—Facebook and LinkedIn.

These two social media platforms hold very different audiences and purposes. Most notably, LinkedIn functions purely as a professional space. If you are working on a B2B (business to business) community or looking to reach professionals, LinkedIn might be the right space for you. However, due to its universality and sheer volume of users (I'm talking billions of active users of Facebook versus just hundreds of millions for LinkedIn), Facebook is likely going to be the logical choice for most community leaders.

Facebook first announced Community Pages (now called Community Groups) in 2010 as a feature designed to address fan pages that were being forced to set up official business pages as there were no other options. In their own words: "Community

Pages are a new type of Facebook Page dedicated to a topic or experience that is owned collectively by the community connected to it. Just like Official Pages for businesses, organizations, and public figures, Community Pages let you connect with others who share similar interests and experiences."

One of the biggest draws for community leaders is that most of your members are already likely to be using the platform. This means you need to simply put your focus on being visible and active, enticing new members to join your group via a simple click of the "join" button.

There are also lots of helpful features from setting rules, running "lives," and setting up event pages, with new things added regularly by Facebook.

There are some major downsides to using a social media platform as the hub of your community that you should bear in mind. The main one is that you don't own your community. You are at the mercy of a huge multi-billion-dollar organization that can change the rules or algorithms with a click of a button and without even letting you know. This can be a bit scary when you've worked so hard to build your membership, as well as frustrating when rules or interfaces suddenly change overnight. However, it's worth remembering that social media platforms want to help you. It's in their favor that your community succeeds and is active because that means more engaged and active users for them, too. So, while this shouldn't stop you from setting up a group, it should spur you to ensure you have some insurance—a backup that gives you more ownership and direct communication with your members. The best way to do this is to collect email addresses from your members when they join (more on that later).

You are also not going to have a huge amount of control over the interface and branding of your community. This might not be a bad thing though. It means that members joining will intuitively know how to use your community space and the recognizable interface might help build familiarity and trust.

Growing an online community on LinkedIn Groups: GIL KOCHAVI, FOUNDER OF DATA-DRIVEN AND DIGITAL MARKING AND LINKERS

Gil Kochavi runs two popular business groups for Israelis. The first is Data-Driven and Digital Marking, which launched in 2014 to connect marketing, digital, and data professionals to help them understand each other's professional world and to help them learn and deploy data-driven methodologies. After seeing a growth in LinkedIn members, Gil also went on to launch Linkers with a partner (Tomer Zuker)—a group for knowledge sharing in regards to using LinkedIn.

Both groups have seen good growth, and Gil puts this down to his engagement activities, which he categories into four pillars:

- **Knowledge**: from global LinkedIn experts, LinkedIn employees, and community members.
- **Networking**: via digital and physical events.
- **Belonging**: community badge, personalization, and members empowerment.

- **Giving**: get support, help others, social giving to chosen voluntary associations, and mentorships programs.

Gil carries out a number of activities in the group to meet these pillars including:

- **Ongoing activities**: welcoming new members, weekly summary (sharing the best-selected posts from the last week), weekly member spotlight, and anonymous questions.
- **Special activities**: education and networking events, refer-a-friend activities, women's months, community milestones, holidays, and the like.
- **Awarding**: top contributors and end-of-year parade for best posts.
- **Communications**: via email, SMS, and WhatsApp (using marketing automation).

Gil wanted to grow professional communities. With most of his target audience being LinkedIn users this was the obvious space to launch his group. He is upfront about the fact that he isn't entirely happy with the platform but acknowledges that changes are happening, "I'm not happy with the current group functionality on LinkedIn. LinkedIn groups product team is aware of the gaps though and are focusing on improving groups functionality.

"I'm a member in LinkedIn groups advisory program, and I am part of the thinking process in defining and designing the new features."

Gil's three biggest community-building tips:

- Define a clear strategy and execute it.
- Manage the group actively on a daily basis.
- Listen to your community members' needs and dreams.

Find out more about Data-Driven and Digital Marketing:
linkedin.com/groups/8178837/
Find out more about Linkers:
linkedin.com/groups/8948621/

STAY UP-TO-DATE WITH YOUR PLATFORM

If you choose to exist on a community-specific platform or social media site, make sure you stay up-to-date with features and changes. I follow many social media experts and influencers who do the hard work for me—sharing updates and tips they've picked up.

If you do settle on Facebook, I'd also suggest getting to know their "community hub" (facebook.com/community), which is intended as a supportive and learning space for group admins and moderators. It's worth joining their mailing list as occasionally there are opportunities and funding available for Facebook communities.

SETTING THE GROUP TO PRIVATE

You will have to decide if you want your group space to be private or public. Backplane was a startup that specialized in creating social networks for brands and celebrity icons. After their success building a fan-based network for Lady Gaga, the company would roll out what they called the "Lady Gaga Playbook" for creating effective online communities. In an article for *Forbes* titled "The Five Rules All Effective Online Communities Must Follow," they share that the first rule is simply: "keep it closed." Your members need to feel comfortable being personal in your community space, so keeping it private is vital.

"That walled garden allows freedom of expression," says Scott Harrison, former president of Backplane. "This is important because people have different personas in different facets of life—whether it's at Littlemonsters (a Lady Gaga fan), a school, a church, or an office environment."

(You are probably also wondering what the other four rules are alongside keeping the community closed. They are:

1. Start small
2. Reward the faithful
3. Let the community define and divide itself
4. An effective online community is an effective offline community.)

HAVING A WEBSITE AND NEWSLETTER

I can't recommend enough having a website and a newsletter for your online community alongside your community hub. The website will act as the face and library of your brand. While the hub will be relevant, fast-moving and user-driven, your website can be controlled and consistent. You can explain clearly what your community is about and why members should join. Showcase all the great benefits members can access. Share upcoming events and useful resources such as blogs, podcasts, or photo galleries. A website will make you look serious and professional, which might not seem important in the beginning but, as you grow, could really help you tap into benefits such as sponsorship or funding.

It doesn't need to be a complex site but it does need to look good and be consistent with your branding colors and logo. It's very easy building a basic website yourself using a theme on WordPress or a website-building service such as Wix or Squarespace.

In addition to the website, you should be collecting emails for a newsletter from the day you launch. Do this even if you don't have the time or inclination to start a newsletter yet! Those emails will become your *most valuable commodity*. Unlike social media, they are in your control and the most direct and versatile method of communicating that you will ever own. Every time you post on social media or in a forum, only a small percentage of your group will see it. A newsletter, however, will have a much wider reach—directly hitting the inbox of your members.

Make sure you are collecting emails or any similar data in line with data collection laws (using a service such as MailChimp to collect emails can help ensure you are doing so correctly). Think about the best way to collect email addresses, for the most part, you'll want to do this as soon as a member joins at a time when they are actively engaged and eager to be involved. I invite new members to subscribe when they join the community and also run occasional giveaways or reveal big announcements in newsletters first to entice others to sign up or stay subscribed as they don't want to miss out.

It's also a good idea to send a welcome email to your new member. This is your chance to showcase your community, give them a sense of your culture and purpose, and point them in the direction of things they might be able to get involved with.

SENDING OUT NEWSLETTERS

While consistency is great for building an audience and engagement, sending an irregular newsletter is better than sending none at all. Keep them short and interesting. See if there's a way you can add value to your members by including links to other relevant articles, sharing videos, or pointing them in the direction of relevant opportunities.

One mistake that I often see with community newsletters is that they are really dry! This is a space for you to speak to your members, so make it personal and engaging. As much as possible, look for ways to bring your community into the newsletter in the form of photos, updates, quotes, or even by highlighting specific posts or a member.

If you need a fantastic example of how to do this, sign up to the Girls' Night In newsletter (girlsnightin.co). Set up by Alisha Ramos when she was looking for a creative outlet, the newsletter focuses simply on "downtime" and has grown to over 140,000 subscribers. Sent out every Friday, you'll receive a personal introduction from Alisha followed by ideas of things to watch, memes, and videos to make you laugh, as well as recipes and interesting articles—all in a beautiful, easy-to-read format. Alisha has done an incredible job of harnessing a sense of community. As well as highlighting quotes or interesting emails she receives from readers, she regularly sends out surveys and asks readers to share opinions on topics. In a subsequent email, she'll share some of the feedback she receives.

WHAT ADDITIONAL PLATFORMS WILL YOU HAVE?

You've got your main hub for your community decided, but you might not want to stop there. Having supporting platforms alongside can act as great communication tools to keep members engaged or share updates with a wider audience of supporters (who might not be in your private group but might want to follow or share your content). Included in this is a Facebook Page which you might want to have as well as your Facebook Group for messaging, and posting in the group under your brand name rather than your personal account and for announcing things publicly.

It can be tempting to sign up to them all—Snapchat, TikTok, Clubhouse, and others—but each platform represents time and effort in maintaining and monitoring, so think logically about your decision. Do your research into the different options and find what your demographic is mostly using. This is where you should focus your energy.

WHAT IS YOUR INCLUSIVITY POLICY?

As a community leader, you are responsible for ensuring your group is inclusive and diverse and making sure all members' voices are being represented. This is an important task and something all organizations are (rightly) being called up on more than ever before, so not something you should overlook. Inclusivity is a big topic and something that you should dedicate time and an open-minded attitude to getting right. You may want to look into getting some training or reading up on the topic so that you are better informed.

To get started, here are a few basic steps that you should be consciously taking:

- Ensure your branding, language, and photos are inclusive.
- Share diverse stories in your content and posts.
- Recruit team members and volunteers with diversity in mind and think about providing some form of inclusion training.
- Appoint an inclusion and diversity volunteer or staff member,
- Create an inclusion policy to share in your group and on your website—perhaps even call on an expert to help you put this together.
- Make inclusion and diversity a part of your community's mission.
- Educate your community by sharing reputable resources.
- Ensure your community rules include tolerance and ensure moderators are strict with rule breakers.
- Carry out surveys and start discussions to give your members an opportunity to provide feedback...and make sure you listen to what is being said!
- Support and share like-minded diverse organizations and communities.
- If you are unsure, ask and reach out to organizations that can help you do everything in your power to be a diverse and inclusive community.

LOOKING OUT FOR VULNERABLE MEMBERS

Another responsibility that you need to consider is looking after vulnerable members. Most of us are not mental health doctors or support workers, so it is not our job to provide a service in this field (unless that's the purpose of your tribe!). However, you are building a community, and part of that structure should include looking out for members who could be struggling and using your space to reach out for help. After all, good communities look out for all their members through good times and bad.

In Love Her Wild, we often get women who are having a tough time and, as a community, we pride ourselves on being there to support them as best we can. This often comes in the form of simply reaching out and touching base. Then, if appropriate, point members in the direction of professionals and services that might be able to help them.

I personally found doing a Mental Health First Aid course was a great tool in educating myself in what to look out for while giving me the confidence to know how to handle situations correctly. I've since appointed a moderator who monitors posts and comments and sends messages checking in with members if they feel they might need additional support. We've received incredible feedback from members who have said the compassion and kindness they've received from our volunteers have gone a long way.

LAUNCH! LAUNCH! LAUNCH!

You can take a deep breath—we've covered all the basic foundations of building an online community. By now, your community skeleton should be looking solid, professional, and consistent. You should have a clear idea of what your community is about, how it will look, and who it is for. It's time for the most crucial step…actually launching!

While I've spent a lot of time in this chapter covering different topics and planning, it's also important to find a balance with this. You'll never feel fully ready to launch, and getting caught up on perfection can be a great distraction technique for stopping yourself from actually taking that terrifying leap and going public. At some point you are going to have to just go for it.

Don't quietly launch your group, saying to yourself you'll talk about it slowly over the coming weeks and months. It's much more effective to set a date and launch with a bang. Do it on a day when you set aside some time to really market and promote your community (see Chapter 3), even better if you can coincide the launch with an exciting opportunity or in-person event (see Chapter 4). The key with this approach is to create excitement around your group to encourage organic shares, new members, and interactions as early as possible. This is an opportunity to get your brand visible and to create a feeling that your community is going to be something people want to be part of.

If you already have a community set up and running, but this chapter has made you think you want to reshape your community, you might want to consider a relaunch. It can feel quite bold doing a relaunch, but it's actually a great way to build new engagement and to reenergize a group.

A relaunch might include a new mission statement, updating of your logo and visuals, the launch of a new event, or the introduction of a new moderation team. Just like with an initial launch, set aside a date and a time to publicly announce the new changes. Encourage your existing members to get on board with this, and ask them to share on their socials and help spread the word.

A great example of an online community that managed this well is Family Lockdown Tips & Ideas founded by Claire Balkind. In just five weeks of launching the group, which was intended to support parents through the Covid lockdowns, had passed a million members. Before the end of the year and off the back of the online community, Claire had published two books, had won awards, and had been recognized in the national press. As restrictions lifted though, the group needed to evolve to stay relevant. The community rebranded and came back as Family Lowdown—the space for families to go to for tried and tested advice—and has remained as engaged as ever.

TAKE THE LEAP

This will probably be the scariest part of the whole process of launching an online community. It's the part where most get stuck and why there are probably a million brilliant community ideas out there that have never come to fruition.

Don't let yours be one of them!

As psychologist Susan Jeffers shared in her internationally bestselling book *Feel the Fear and Do It Anyway*:

"Often, we think, I'll do it when I'm not so afraid. But in reality, it works the other way round. The doing it comes before the fear goes away. The only way to get rid of the fear of doing something is to go out and do it."

GROWING YOUR COMMUNITY ON SOLID FOUNDATIONS

ARDEN JOY, FOUNDER OF HER ADVENTURES

Travel was something that came later in life for Arden Joy. Growing up in a family with little money, it took her a while to figure everything out and to scrape every penny she had to make it happen. On returning home from her first trip though, Arden was hooked. Traveling had been transformational. She was stronger and more empathetic, able to see that people were more alike than different.

Seeing the barriers stopping women from traveling—including money, discrimination, safety, time, and access—Arden decided to do something about it. She launched a blog titled Her Adventures, a place where she could provide information.

"The blog was nice," Arden explained, "But I knew I needed something more. I wanted to create a space where we could work together to travel and learn from each other. From there, I started the Her Adventures Facebook group and that's when things really took off. Women from over one hundred countries joined and became part of a global effort to help each other to see the world.

"But over the years, travel resources became plentiful as amazing blogs, fun trips, and, of course, wonderful online communities began going strong. Within a few years, women were becoming leaders in the travel industry. At the same time, I began to notice a trend: the dominant voice and thus the very definition of travel itself was almost entirely for people of privilege (i.e. cis, heterosexual, thin, abled, white, strong passport, access to money, etc.). And so, my vision of empowering women began to shift.

"I changed our mission to 'radically redefining travel to be inclusive, empowering, and sustainable' and our tagline to 'explore beyond your boundaries.' Showing that travel can happen any time you explore beyond your boundaries, which can be anything from visiting a new country, to exploring a new neighborhood, to discovering a new place in a book.

"I took the airplane out of our logo and replaced it with a map pin in a heart, to send that message that wherever you are on the map, there are opportunities to travel right there. And together with my team, we began working to lift up underrepresented voices within the group and to provide them with more resources.

"So, all that to say started out as a simple idea for empowering women to learn the basics of travel has turned into a powerful community that's literally changing the face of the travel industry.

"It's been a wild ride, but the only one I'd ever want to be on!"

Alongside a supportive group, the Her Adventures community provides a wealth of resources, which include courses, toolkits, language exchanges, virtual tours, gift exchanges, speakers, and classes. Although Her Adventures has a website, blog, store, podcast, newsletter, and multiple social media platforms, the community "lives" primarily on Facebook. Arden has no doubts that Facebook groups are one of the best decisions for a community to exist due to it being such a community-led space.

Arden says about what the early days of growing her community were like, "I gave it a lot of time, I had a plan, and I made it up as I went along. I went into Her Adventures with a vision and lots and lots of great ideas. But building a community isn't the same as building a typical business. The community drives not just the conversation, but the direction. My vision always remained the same, I wanted to empower women to travel. But how I did that shifted over time because what I thought they needed wasn't always what they actually needed.

"A lot of the early days were spent creating a solid foundation that has kept us strong for many years. I was lucky enough to find a team of women who were as passionate about my vision as I was. We worked, relentlessly, to define ourselves. We developed a mission, a community agreement, a set of promises that we as a community would strive for when we traveled. We developed rules for the community and rules for ourselves as a team. We came up with procedures for addressing everything from disagreements to discrimination to crises. All of those things have grown over time, but the guiding principles and plans remain in place and I am positive are the reason we have succeeded and grown all these years."

Arden recognizes that, like with a lot of things on the internet, luck and timing have a part to play in her journey. But there's a lot more than that going on behind the scenes. Her

Adventures has seen steady growth since launching. Arden has never used advertising so relies entirely on word of mouth. She believes they have good content and a good community that makes people want to tell their friends. With strong community values and the hard work of moderators, Her Adventures has become a safe, sacred space for many of its members.

"We provide a lot of reasons for people to stay engaged. Everything from thought provoking discussions on topics like how to talk about a bad experience without letting it define an entire place, people or culture to fun activities like online scavenger hunts to silly questions like share your favorite travel fail photo."

Arden has also managed to bring together a dedicated team of thirty-five volunteers spanning the globe who help her run the community by moderating the Facebook group, writing blog posts, or managing social media accounts. Some of them approached Arden offering to help, but others she reached out to after noticing how engaged they were with the group, thinking they would be a great fit for the team.

Arden describes the volunteers as her family. Her Adventures wouldn't exist without them! She makes a point of incorporating fun with her team, be it a team meet-up or a virtual escape room. Activities that create downtime, foster self-care, and team bonding.

No matter your community, there are going to be challenges you are going to face along the way. For a travel community, I think it's safe to say that a global pandemic is probably as high as you can get on the problems scale! While many travel organizations were forced to close, Arden showed incredible adaptability and was even able to use the pandemic to tighten her community ethos and sense of support even further:

"Emotions and fears were running high, and we had to make decisions, fast, about what to do with a travel group when people can't travel. After years of preaching that travel can happen anywhere, anytime, that it can be done from home even, we found ourselves called to live our values to the fullest. Within a few weeks of lockdown, we had launched an #ExploreFromHome campaign on Facebook that covered the gamut of exploration. We filled our website with articles about podcasts, recipes, movies, activities and more that were travel themed. We began hosting #ExploreFromHome exchanges, ranging from snacks to souvenirs, all aimed at bringing travel straight to people's doorsteps.

"A moderator, and our resident baker, started doing a Facebook Live baking show called *Desserts Around the World* where she would teach members how to make desserts from different countries using recipes provided by members from that country (hopefully a cookbook will be coming out of this at some point!). We held movie nights, using the Chrome extension Teleparty to meet online and watch films from across the globe from documentaries to rom coms. And we started hosting virtual tours and classes. We did things together like learn meditation from a Buddhist monk in Japan, go on a walking tour of Chernobyl which supported the Dogs of Chernobyl non-profit, and even take a journey inward with a travel themed yoga class.

"Being an admin of a community is a really hard and misunderstood role. As the leader, you tend to mostly deal with the problems that arise. Disgruntled members or website outages, whatever it is, you're usually involved. And it can get exhausting and demoralizing. After all, you just wanted to create a community for something you're passionate about, not sit around on a holiday weekend trying to resolve an issue in the community that's going south quickly.

"It can be easy to wonder if you're cut out for all this and if it's worth it. I can tell you that you are, and it is. The reason your community is thriving is because of you. But you need to recognize that and protect yourself so you can come back and keep going. Rely on others for help. Recognize that not every problem needs to be addressed immediately (or at all!). Make sure you build in time away from your community when you won't check your phone or answer emails. Give yourself the chance to remember why you started your community in the first place."

Arden's three biggest community-building tips:

- Remember that a community isn't about numbers, it's about, well, community. Sometimes it's easy to think that the best community is a big one. But there's no numerical value to a community of people who feel connected to each other and to you. If you're only focused on numbers, you're missing the point of community.
- Be genuine, vulnerable, and transparent. You don't need to be an influencer or a marketer to grow a community. If you want to gain trust and grow followers, be your authentic self. Admit when you make mistakes, ask for help, be open about what you're doing, and address issues face on.
- Surround yourself with trusted advisors. When you build your team, make sure that they're people who don't just agree with you. Invite people with perspectives, ideas, experiences, and beliefs that are different

than yours, and make sure they know their voice is important, and that they are part of guiding you and the community.

Find out more about Her Travels:
heradventures.com
@ardenjoy and @girlswhotravel

CHAPTER 2

LEAD THE WAY

In 2016 when I decided to hike the length of Israel, I also started a blog. I created a basic WordPress site and called it The Ordinary Adventurer. I'd always wanted a blog to call my own but, for too many years, I told myself my writing wasn't good enough. This stemmed from my school days when undiagnosed dyslexia meant I struggled in classes, often feeling stupid and like I couldn't keep up with my classmates. My dream of being an author was mocked (quite literally by my English teacher, "How do you expect to be a writer one day if you can't even do basic spelling?"), so I learned to hide my work from others.

It took doing a 1,000 km hike to give myself permission to finally launch a blog. I could tell others I was simply doing it to keep a journal of my adventure.

While on the hike, my blog began to grow in popularity along with my social media platforms, which I'd set up to share my blog posts and photos along the way. I began sharing tips I'd picked up and advice on wild camping and hiking. I did my first podcast interview and, on returning from the hike, I gave my first talk, designed to inspire others to go on their own adventures.

I didn't know it at the time, but this was the beginning of my growing what is known as a personal brand. Personal branding is pitching yourself as an authority in your industry, increasing your credibility, influence, and career. As the title of my blog suggests, I was building authority as an adventurer but from the perspective of someone with little experience or expertise. And, as my following increased, so did the opportunities such as sponsorship offers and paid talks.

When I launched Love Her Wild (which came about ten months after starting my blog), I shared this in a blog post and on my social media platforms. There wasn't much thought involved, but it just made sense for me to do this.

From the beginning, I have always been very visible in the group. It wouldn't take new members long to see that Love Her Wild was launched by "Bex Band"—my personal brand. There's a video of me pinned to the top of the Facebook group welcoming new members. Any newsletters or emails are signed off by me personally. I have intertwined my journey into the story of Love Her Wild; on the website homepage it reads how I came to the decision to launch the community:

"It wasn't until my mid-twenties that I started going on adventures, and it wasn't easy at first. I found the outdoors to be male-dominant, competitive and judgmental. I felt I didn't belong. So, I set up a women's adventure community, Love Her Wild, to create a different kind of space. One that was kind, supportive, and focused on having fun, not simply reaching a goal."

All these things happened very organically, but I can see how having a personal brand and being a visible leader has benefited the community greatly. It gave the community authority and opened up opportunities that simply wouldn't have existed without my personal input and story driving its launch. It also made it *much* easier to get exposure for Love Her Wild. Podcasts, journalists, brands, talks, and collaborations... they don't want to work with a name, they want a person.

Being a visible leader has also helped make Love Her Wild more personable. It's given the community a face, someone that members recognize and can reach out to if they have queries or a problem. Being upfront about the reasons I set up the community makes it more relatable and emotive. Everyone loves a story. If you've got one, use it!

My personal brand also provided me with an income while I focused on establishing Love Her Wild; the community wasn't yet making any money. Through delivering talks and writing articles and books, I was able to sell my expertise, freeing up my time to grow the group to what it is today. It took away the pressure of having to monetize the community too soon, making decisions based on financial need rather than what was right for Love Her Wild.

There's another huge benefit to having a personal brand that I think is important to mention. It's why I'd always recommend taking the same route I did (of having your own platform/s alongside your community) versus just being visible and named within your group. And here's why: as we've already established, you are going to work *really, really* hard to grow your online community. You are going to put in the hours. Work through the struggles. Use all your good ideas and knock down every door you can find to make it work. Having a personal brand protects all that hard work. It's your insurance card and maybe even your ticket to freedom at a later date. There might be a time when you no longer want to run the group any more, or perhaps you just want to lessen your involvement and work on something new. With a personal brand, stepping away won't mean losing all those hours you put into growing the community and building trust because you will take away your own personal followers. You can keep your platform—and as a personal platform, it's yours to do as you please and pivot any which direction you like. If you grew a tattoo-enthusiast community but now you want to run poetry workshops, then so be it!

Being so visible in a community wasn't always a comfortable decision. I was lacking in confidence launching the community, so it would have been a lot easier to do this if I was hiding behind a name and logo. There was no doubt that if the community failed, that was my failure to own. That was quite a nerve-wracking feeling to overcome.

I also spent a lot of time (needlessly) worrying about being seen as wanting to make the community about me. I've always been eager to make the group diplomatic and fair, and I worried that taking a leadership role would look a bit "me, me, me." In time, I've realized that having leadership is essential to decision-making and keeping a tribe moving towards its purpose. There's no shame in stepping up and taking that role. If led well and from a good place, it doesn't prevent your community from being a collaborative space, it will only help support this.

There's a lot of fun that comes with being a visible leader of a community and having a personal brand. Like going to a Love Her Wild event where everyone knows who you are (I can't get used to that one!) or being invited to an all-paid-for "influencer retreat" by a big brand for my work celebrating getting women outdoors (yes please!). It hasn't all been a positive experience though. One of the most painful challenges to deal with was negative comments and trolls online. When you are providing a face and a name, this will be directed to you. It's impossible to not take them personally.

It also comes with a lot more work. To grow a personal brand, you need to be visible on at least one social media platform and need to be putting out regular content around your "authority" topic. Building a following is going to take some time and effort. So, this is a big decision to make and not one to go into without some consideration.

It might be that you can't be the face of your community for whatever reason and that is OK, it's not impossible to still harness trust and grow a successful group. NaNoWriMo (National Novel Writing Month) has helped millions of writers achieve their dreams of writing a novel and function as a supportive community without a clear visible leader.

To help you make the decision, here are the pros and cons to weigh up:

Pros of building a personal brand alongside your community:

- Easier to build a narrative into the community, something that will help attract new members and serve you well when seeking out marketing opportunities and exposure.
- Makes the community more personable and relatable.
- Members will know who to contact or reach out to if they have queries or problems.
- Provides more opportunities and advertisement in the form of interviews on podcasts and the press, collaborations with other public figures, individual awards,

and becoming a spokesperson and point of authority in your industry.

- Supports growth: you can invite your personal brand followers to join your group and vice versa.
- Increases monetization opportunities.
- Can show the "behind-the-scenes" of running a community, and create better connections with your community members.
- Protects your time personally in case, in the future, you want to branch out or explore other initiatives.

Cons of building a personal brand alongside your community:

- More work as you need to juggle additional social media platforms and put out content so you need to be realistic about your time commitments.
- Can make mishaps and challenges feel more personal than if you are hidden behind a brand name.
- This can put more of a strain on your time and energy; as your community grows, you will likely get more members asking you questions or wanting to spend time with you.

GROWING A PERSONAL BRAND

I could fill a whole other book sharing my experience on growing a personal brand. Really though, I can see five key components that I think have been key to my success:

1. Find your authentic voice

According to John Jantsch, author of *Duct Tape Marketing: The World's Most Practical Small Business Marketing Guide,*

"Personal branding is the art of becoming knowable, likeable, and trustable." He talks a lot in the book about the importance of being authentic. Based on my own experience, I can't emphasize this enough! People are drawn to vulnerability and honesty. Being an authority doesn't mean you have to know everything. You will be trusted far more if you are honest about what you know and bring the audience along with your learning and the failures along the way.

In an industry full of chiseled photos and rugged adventurers achieving huge feats, I stood out as an inexperienced adventurer lacking in confidence who went the color of a tomato every time she exercised and wasn't afraid to share when things went wrong. I know my followers appreciate that I don't try to gloss over my truth!

2. Put out content that is either SEO smart or interesting

I regularly put out content on my authority topic: adventure and the outdoors. I chose to focus on blog posts and social media posts (which are shared on my Instagram and Facebook pages) mostly because I love writing. You might find you'd enjoy doing a podcast or making YouTube films more. It doesn't matter what form it takes but, as always, choose something you enjoy or you won't keep it up.

As much as possible, I put an emphasis on content being interesting rather than worrying about putting out a post "every Tuesday afternoon." If I've not got exciting adventures to share or great tips to pass on, I prefer to stay quiet. This increases my chances of keeping engagement up and means posts are more likely to be shared and relevant to my audience.

In time, I also developed one of my valuable skills: learning about Search Engine Optimization (SEO), which is the process of improving content to increase traffic, i.e., crafting a blog post so that it appears high up on Google pages when people search for it. Many of my blog posts on useful topics (such as tips for camping or my most recommended hiking backpack) rank highly and drive thousands of readers to my blog every month. Once there, I can scoop some of them up as followers or newsletter subscribers or can encourage them to join the Love Her Wild community.

You can use the same skills to apply effective SEO to YouTube videos or podcasts. To learn more on SEO, I would recommend reading *3 Months to No. 1: The "No-Nonsense" SEO Playbook for Getting Your Website Found on Google* by Will Coombe. Once you've got a good understanding of SEO and are ready to find some potential good keywords (words and phrases that people are searching regularly), I'd suggest using either Keysearch or Semrush.

3. Network nonstop

Putting out content alone is rarely enough (unless you get insanely lucky—like Matt Coyne who launched his Man versus Baby brand off the back of a single viral post about being a new father). You are also probably going to have to do some networking. I did this in a number of ways. The first was commenting in forums or joining in discussions online with other public figures or enthusiasts in my industry.

I also attended many physical networking opportunities. Including going to relevant exhibitions and events and even business networking meet-ups (you'll be amazed by the opportunities that present themselves when you start chatting to people and passing out business cards!). I made it my goal to meet many people, online or offline, making sure to mention who I was and what I was working on.

4. Put yourself forward as a spokesperson

You've got to be brave and put yourself forward as an authority in your field. That doesn't mean you think you are the biggest expert on the topic; of course, there will be others who know more than you. What it does mean is that you think you are a good communicator and have an interesting opinion on the topic that others might relate to.

One of the best ways to get your voice heard as an authority is by providing quotes and interviews for journalists. It might be that you are running a community for blind football players and building a personal brand alongside this as a spokesperson for accessible sports. So, when you see a journalist is writing a topic on a sport in your area, it's a great chance for you to put yourself forward and to provide a quote. To find these journalists' requests look for groups that connect media with spokespeople. Examples are the helpareporter.com (HARO) website or the Lightbulb - Entrepreneur Press and Hangout Facebook group. I've also had a lot of success from simply searching #JourrnoRequest on Twitter and skimming through the latest requests from journalists.

5. Don't be shy to get recognized for your work

There are so many awards out there all looking for individuals to celebrate, and maybe you could be one of them! Winning awards has provided me with brilliant exposure and led to many interviews where I can shout about my community. It also really helps to support my image as an authority figure.

Dedicate some time to looking on web searches to find appropriate awards to apply for. Try to find niche categories you might fit into—women in businesses, local community heroes, or LGBTQ+ influencers—or any awards around your authority topic.

Like with many of the skills in this book, you'd benefit greatly from gaining a wider understanding of the topic. There have been some great books written about growing a personal brand, these are just some of my favorites:

- *Crush It!: Why NOW Is the Time to Cash In on Your Passion* by Gary Vaynerchuk (HarperStudio, 2009)
- *I Am My Brand: How to Build Your Brand Without Apology* by Kubi Springer (Bloomsbury Business, 2019)
- *Brand You: Turn Your Unique Talents into a Winning Formula* by David Royston-Lee and John Purkiss (Pearson, 2012)
- *Influencer: Building Your Personal Brand in the Age of Social Media* by Brittany Hennessy (Citadel, 2018)

BUILDING A PERSONAL BRAND ALONGSIDE A COMMUNITY

HELEN COLEBROOK, FOUNDER OF JOURNAL WITH PURPOSE

You might think that to have a personal brand you need to be a loud and overly confident individual. Someone who would jump at the chance of being in front of the camera. Helen Colebrook's story proves that this isn't the case!

Her journey is one that shows the great benefits of building trust and connections over time as an authority in your field and how that can serve you when you are launching a community. Helen has overcome her Imposter syndrome and now runs Journal with Purpose full-time.

Helen loves journaling, and seven years ago, she began sharing her pages online in journaling forums and groups. Over a period of time, people started to ask her for tutorials on writing topics and to share her creative techniques. This led to her setting up a blog and YouTube channel. As her connection with her followers deepened, she understood more about their needs and became committed to launching an online community to support these further. She launched the Journal with Purpose

Journaling Club, whose mission is "to help people improve their lives immeasurably, through journaling, planning and creativity."

Members can join via Patreon (patreon.com)—a subscription platform—and in return receive benefits such as monthly journal prompts, tutorials, creative challenges, and access to a private member's Facebook group. The more money members pledge the more benefits they receive.

"In the very early days of launching I had no plan at all," Helen explained. "I just wanted to connect with people and share my passion. I probably didn't spend more than fifteen minutes a day working on it. In a way, I think this did me a favor as I had no motive and nothing to 'sell,' just a desire to feel connected.

"Once my community really started growing, I decided to start putting together a more structured plan as I could see there were some wonderful possibilities ahead. I was being contacted by people asking for more in-depth help and also receiving messages from businesses that wanted to work with me. At that point, I thought 'I might be onto something here!'"

Despite offering paid-for courses on her website alongside the subscription costs for joining her community, Helen still gives a lot of content for free via her channels. It's this regular content that has helped her build a name for herself as a go-to for journaling. When I asked her what her advice is for growing a personal brand, she replied, "I think it's really important to take time getting to know your field, connecting with others and getting a feel for who your ideal audience/customer is. I loved my early days of just sharing online, chatting with people who were interested, and finding new and inspiring people to follow online. I think this has served my personal brand well as my audience know that being connected and inspiring others is at the heart of what I do.

"When you have a personal brand, I think it's important to be authentic, show some of your personal side as well as your business, be kind to others, and avoid getting involved in any heated online spats! I've seen so many people damage their brands by not learning when to walk away from online bullies.

"I also believe strongly in continuing to grow and develop myself. I am always signing up to online classes and reading books that I think will help me serve my audience in better ways."

The combination of her personal brand and online community has allowed Helen to pursue a career sharing her passion for journaling. Like many community leaders, her income is spread across different revenues. Currently, Patreon accounts for 30 percent, online courses 30 percent, collaborations 20 percent, book royalties 15 percent, and shop sales 5 percent. Other than helping with editing her videos, she manages the community and content by herself.

Pursuing this as a career has, of course, come with challenges. One of them is keeping up the battle of attracting new members and keeping existing members engaged. Offerings are made really clear on the website and on social media so that visitors can easily know what's available. Helen also makes a point to ask her members what they want so that what she's providing is of value.

Being in front of the camera also wasn't easy for Helen. "I have had some really big confidence issues along the way," she shared. "They mainly showed up as being scared to show my face on camera and also 'imposter syndrome.' I have joined a creative entrepreneur's hub online, which has been really helpful with business stuff such as marketing plans, email list building, creating a website and building a brand, but the more personal issues are things I have tackled myself. I set myself a challenge to film myself on camera every week for twenty weeks, and by the end, a lot of that early fear had left me. Dealing with imposter syndrome is an ongoing journey, but I try not to let it hold me back."

Helen's three biggest community-building tips:

- Take time to get to know and connect with your ideal audience in a genuine way before jumping in with products or services you want to offer. Too much selling will put up a barrier that is very hard to get past. Think about how you can help your community rather than what you would like to get out of the community.
- Don't worry too much about all the technical side of an online community. You can definitely learn each stage as you go, and there are lots of technical "how-to" videos on YouTube.
- Make sure you listen to your audience. I regularly put out polls, and people love telling you what they would like to see from you. It's one of the most valuable and free resources out there.

Find out more about Journal with Purpose:
journalwithpurpose.co.uk
@journalwithpurpose

CHAPTER 3

GROW YOUR TRIBE

Welcome to the stage of community building that I call... hustling!

I find it strange now that I was always considered somewhat of a quitter. Many times in my life, I remember being told by others that I quit too soon and can't stick things out. I was one of those children (and then adults) who had a million ideas and would constantly be starting something new but never see them through to the end. With Love Her Wild, though, it was different.

When I returned from the Israel hike, I had ahead of me the luxury of free time. My husband and I had saved a few thousand pounds each to do the hike, but it had come in much cheaper than either of us had planned. So rather than rushing back to our previous jobs in London, we decided to see how long we could stretch the remainder of our savings. It seemed logical to base ourselves in cheap countries (Tanzania and then Honduras) where we could prolong our traveling as long as possible.

Despite the call of beaches and backpacker bars, I remained fiercely focused on my new projects. Finding cafes or lobbies with free internet, I'd work on my blog and grow my personal brand, occasionally doing sponsored posts or paid articles—my first taste of earning money off my own back. Most of my time, however, was spent on Love Her Wild. Working with an intensity that I'd never experienced before.

I had no idea where I was heading with the group or if it would even amount to anything, but that didn't matter. I was excited and enjoyed the challenge. It was fun watching something grow from nothing and being the one responsible for that.

I heeded the advice of self-development author and speaker, Brian Tracy, who said, "Do something every day that moves you one step forward toward your major goal." This quote really stuck with me. I spent every spare waking hour hustling. Consuming stories and knowledge shared online in blogs and YouTube channels. Thinking up new ways to market the community and get its name out there. Putting myself forward for podcasts and interviews. Suggesting collaborations. Chatting with members in the group. Connecting with potential new members in forums and other groups. Chasing every opportunity I could find. Creating content and scheduling posts. Thinking up new ways to engage members. Sending out dozens of emails a day, even if just to introduce myself to someone of interest.

Every day, I was throwing everything at the wall that I could think of, hoping that something would stick. The failures and rejections were in their masses, but I'd hold on to the small wins. I soon realized that my next "yes" was just a few failures away.

In time, my hard work began to pay off. Often the growth would be so slow and the fruits of my labor so minimal, it was easy to miss. But each month I could look back and see that numbers had risen; engagement was on the up and good things had happened.

The feeling this gave me was like nothing else I'd worked on before, especially when the trickle of messages came in from women saying thank you for the group or sharing how it'd helped them in some way—be it making a new friend or giving them the confidence to make a dream happen. I bottled that feeling and turned it into motivation, drive, and determination.

There's an element of trust in the process of growing your online community. Because, for the majority of us, there is no quick fix or easy path. Success will come from a sum of a lot of small steps in the general direction to where you want to go. At times, I would often compare this to the feeling of swimming against the tide. It was a constant fight to keep on top of the group admin while also chasing every avenue to market the community and keep members engaged.

Until, one day, the tide shifted. It was slow at first but then suddenly very noticeable. It was all falling into place. That doesn't mean the challenges ended (I've accepted as a community leader that dealing with problems will always be part of the role!), but it does mean that you won't have to hustle so hard forever. It's a strange formula but in anything you do (whether it is working with money, or talking about followings in groups, or attendees at events) numbers really do grow numbers. So, the growth of your community will be self-serving. Opportunities will start knocking on your door, and growth will happen more organically. You might even start to find yourself in a position that I am in now where I regularly turn away interviews, sponsorships, or collaborations because I simply get too many offers now and can't work with them all. What a great position to be in!

When you stop believing that your hard work will result in a thriving online community, then you will lose hope. Without hope, you will have no motivation. Your efforts and community will fizzle out.

Make sure that doesn't happen to you.

Set yourself targets. Work to a schedule if that's how you get things done. Keep sending emails and putting yourself out there. Don't ever stop innovating or trying new things (this is an important one!). Embrace the rejections and failures—they are a fabric of literally *all* success stories. When no one would sign him rapper Jay-Z took matters into his own hands launching Roc-a-Fella Records and, after releasing his own debut album *Reasonable Doubt*, he is now one of the world's bestselling music artists selling over 125 million records. Author Stephen King's first book was rejected by over thirty publishers. Even J.K. Rowling's *Harry Potter* book was rejected twelve times before being published. As the well-known American life and business strategist Tony Robbins said:

"There are no real successes without rejection. The more rejection you get, the better you are, the more you've learned, the closer you are to your outcome…. If you can handle rejection, you'll learn to get everything you want."

So, it's time to start taking those small steps and to start chasing rejections. When building an online community, this comes down to three crucial focuses: attract new members, keep existing members engaged, and alongside these both, ensure you maintain your community culture.

STEPS YOU CAN TAKE TO HELP GROW YOUR COMMUNITY:

Of course, a lot of your focus will be on attracting new members, especially early on. Use some of the below techniques to get your community visible and to encourage numbers to grow in your group.

Invite your friends and family to join your community

This really should be the first thing you do once you've launched your online community. Many platforms have an "invite" option where you can directly send a notification to your network. Alongside this, I'd also recommend writing an email to all your contacts (be brave!) saying what your community is about and, crucially, asking if they mind sharing a post and passing it on to their own friends and family. The people you know are going to be your biggest fans initially, so make sure you utilize that as much as possible and don't be shy asking for their help.

Share in other groups

One of the best ways to reach your target audience is in existing communities and groups. You'll need to check what the posting rules are in each group but, if allowed, you can post about your community inviting people to join. This is often best done if you can create a post that doesn't look like a simple blank advert for the group. For example, you could start a relevant discussion or share a giveaway or opportunity that your community is running that also includes a link for anyone to join if they are interested.

It's also effective to join in discussions where you can mention your community if relevant to a topic or question that has been posted.

71

Write guest blogs or interviews

This can take a bit of time so is best done as a back-burner task. In the beginning of launching Love Her Wild, I'd try to write one guest blog or interview a week. The key is to reach out to websites and blogs that have a similar target audience as yours. Offer to write a relevant blog post or to conduct an interview if they are happy to send you questions. They will get free content for their site and, in return, you will get an opportunity to talk about your community and to include a link in your article (if possible, put the link to your website—not to your community hub; this is because you then get what is called a "backlink," which can support the authority of your website).

You are going to get a lot of ignored emails and rejections, so you'll need to approach this systematically. Create a big spreadsheet with all the possible websites and keep a note of the ones you have contacted.

Put yourself forward as a podcast guest

Podcasters are always on the lookout for new guests. Find as many relevant podcasts as you can (again, you want to focus on ones that will have a similar target audience) and send an email saying you think you'd be a great fit for their listeners (often you'll find a "contact me" section if they have a website, otherwise just simply drop them a message on their social media pages).

The podcaster won't pick you if they think you are only interested in advertising your community, so try to attach a story to your pitch: it could be something personal, your own journey that got you to where you are now, or an interesting topic you can discuss and provide insight on.

Send out a press release

Getting an article in the paper, an interview in a magazine, or a mention on the radio is great free advertising for your community. Create a press release for the launch of your community (use Google to find a press release template that you can use as a guide). Your press release is going to need an interesting hook or story—this could be your personal story or maybe something topical such as your community launching because it is needed at this specific time.

Collect the contact details for relevant magazines, papers, and radio, which can usually be found on the "contact us" page on their websites. Targeting local press will likely have the biggest success rate. (Top tip: you can sometimes pay for journalist and newspaper email lists on fiverr.com, which will save you a huge amount of time trying to collect these yourself.)

Recruit your members to help spread the word

In your community hub or in newsletters, you should regularly be asking members to invite their friends and family to join the group. Also think about running occasional campaigns where you ask members to share photos on their profile that talk about the community and invite others to join. This could work well if you run it as a competition (i.e., members sharing their best "meet-up" photo on their personal profiles).

STEPS YOU CAN TAKE TO KEEP COMMUNITY ENGAGEMENT:

While finding new members is an important task, keeping your existing ones engaged should not be overlooked. There's no point putting effort into finding ten new members if ten existing members leave because they feel the group is dormant or not relevant to them anymore.

Keeping engagement requires providing constant value within the group and ensuring that every single one of your members feels welcomed and important. There are a number of ways you can do this:

Welcome new members

You want to leave a great first impression when new members join and to immediately make them feel a part of your community. There are a few ways you can do this. You could send them a direct message introducing yourself and explaining what they can expect from being in the group. You could do a weekly post where you publicly welcome new members and invite them to introduce themselves (tag them if possible so they see it). Another way to ensure a friendly welcome is to make sure the "about me" section or your feature post (the post that appears first on your community hub) is welcoming. I created a welcome video where I introduce myself and the community and have this pinned to the top of our main Facebook group so it's the first thing members see.

Create recurring discussion posts

Activity feeds activity, so it's important that you encourage engagement in your group. If using a social media platform as your hub, this will also help your group to be seen by more people outside of your community as algorithms tend to favor and advertise active groups over quiet ones. To encourage engagement, think about weekly posts you can put in the group that will spark discussions. This could be inviting members to share an achievement from that week or something you have done or created recently, asking for their thoughts on a relevant topic, doing a poll to gauge general opinions, or asking what their favorite bit of gear/song/recipe/game is—just make sure it's relevant.

These posts often work well if they occur on the same day each week, and for most platforms, they can even be scheduled in advance. Posts usually get more traction if they have an image attached. You could use the same image or photo each time so members become familiar with this being a recurring post (remember to use something that is in keeping with your brand's visual identity).

Be an active member

You should lead by example. You hope that your members will become active and engaged in the group, so you should, too. Like posts, join in discussions and leave comments when members share things. This won't go unnoticed by your members and will help you stay familiar with your group's needs and most active members.

Get to know social media algorithms

Put simply, algorithms are technical means of social media platforms sorting and prioritizing posts for users. You'll want to have a basic understanding of algorithms for the social media platforms you use. Often this is just a guessing game, followed by learning what has worked well for your group and what hasn't.

Knowing algorithms will ensure that your time spent posting isn't wasted and will be seen by lots of your members, increasing the chances of engagement. For example, you might post an update in the group first thing in the morning but find that you get no likes or comments. If you had understood algorithms, you'd know that posting the same thing at lunchtime (a much more popular time for social media users) with an image (which most algorithms favor) and finishing with a question (encouraging engagement which in turn boosts your chances of being seen) is likelier to be seen by a lot more members.

Different target audiences will be accessing social media at different times of the day. So, it's important that you understand popular times in your group by using the "insights" feature that you will find on most social media platforms. This will tell you the most popular times and days for your group. You can also experiment a bit—using different types of posts and at different times—to see what gets the most amount of likes and comments.

Look for milestones to celebrate

For any tribe or community, celebrations are a great opportunity to boost morale and positivity. This could be a simple post of gratitude or acknowledgement, or you could tie it in with a giveaway or a real-life meet-up. You could celebrate big community milestones such as anniversaries or passing certain numbers. Or you can focus on members and celebrate successes and achievements within the community. Setting up annual awards for the "kindest member" or "funniest post" could give you a great opportunity to highlight and celebrate your most interested members.

Members' appreciation posts also work really well and take the hard work out of you trying to track down members to celebrate. You could do a post asking members to give a shout-out to a member who has helped them that month with a kind comment, a bit of inspiration, or sharing something funny that made their day. Even better if you can award the nominees with a small prize to show your gratitude such as a pin or a vinyl sticker.

Ask for your members to share their thoughts

Everyone likes to feel heard, and your community members are no different. Do regular polls and surveys and ask questions. Listen to the responses you get and—if you ever decide to act on feedback—make sure you are vocal about this in the group so members feel listened to and like their opinions matter. Listening to feedback is actually a really important way to keep your community engaged and relevant as your viewpoint and opinions will inevitably always be one-sided.

Run giveaways and opportunities

Providing something such as a bit of gear or tickets to an event provides great value to your members and is an effective way to boost engagement and keep members excited about your group. Giveaways can often be fairly easy to organize and just require you to reach out to relevant brands asking for prizes. In exchange, you can offer a photo and tag in the group as part of the competition—a form of advertising for the company (in Chapter 4, I cover how to get sponsorship).

Before running the giveaway, think about how best to maximize on the opportunity to increase engagement in the group or to get members to post publicly in the hope it will drive new members to your page.

Show gratitude to your most active members

If a member is being especially active or supportive in the community, I like to find a way to show my gratitude. I either send them a direct message or sometimes even a postcard in the mail. This lets them know that they are appreciated and will encourage them to remain active and engaged.

STEPS YOU CAN TAKE TO MAINTAIN COMMUNITY CULTURE:

While it can be easy to put all your focus into growing and maintaining members, it's vital that you don't overlook implementing community culture. It's here that your ethos is set and your members will gel. The space you create and the way you show up in your group determines the community culture and the soul of any tribe. It's driven by you at the top and then your representatives if you choose to bring on volunteers or staff.

As Peter Block says in *Community: The Structure of Belonging*, "The key to creating or transforming community…is to see the power in the small but important elements of being with others. The shift we seek needs to be embodied in each invitation we make, each relationship we encounter, and each meeting we attend. For at the most operational and practical level, after all the thinking about policy, strategy, mission, and milestones, it gets down to this: How are we going to be when we gather together?"

Be yourself

Although as leaders you sometimes need to have your "serious hat" on, this doesn't mean you can't also relax and be yourself within your community. Letting your personality shine through invites your members to also show up and be their authentic selves. It's from here that wonderful friendships can form.

Lean into kindness

Being kind is a rule in Love Her Wild as well as being part of our ethos. At the beginning of any event, we remind attendees to be kind and regularly look for ways to encourage this online. Most importantly though, all our leaders embody this principle, showing kindness to all of our members (even the most testing ones!). I'd encourage you to do the same.

I've led enough expeditions in my time to know that fostering kindness is the single most effective way to form a strong team bond and firm friendships. There aren't many spaces left in the world that feel entirely safe and supportive, so let your community be one of those exceptional few.

Enforce and manage group rules

We've already covered that having rules will help protect and foster a safe space and prevent your hub from simply being abused for promotional purposes. There's no point having rules though if they aren't going to be enforced. Make sure you have clear steps in place for rule breakers. In Love Her Wild, rule breakers usually receive a warning and are told that if they break the rules again they will be removed from the community. In some cases (like if someone was to share incredibly offensive views) there is no warning, and members are removed and banned immediately. You will be well respected by your community if you can show strong leadership when it comes to enforcing rules.

After a couple of years of running my community group, I started to develop a bit of a sixth sense to posts that are going to spark conflict. I'd always pay close attention to any comments on these and would try to step in before any big arguments broke out. You can do this by stopping comments on the post or taking it down entirely (although you want to be careful not to offend the original poster by doing this, so make sure you also speak with them directly if you do take this step so they understand your reasoning). Sometimes simply reminding members to stay friendly and kind in the comments is enough to stop arguments from escalating.

Reach out to members when conflict arises

In the instance that conflicts and arguments break out, it's a good idea to open direct communication with those involved. You might need to do this to anyone who has broken rules, but you should also be doing it to anyone who has been on the receiving end of hate or aggression. Simply check in to see if they are OK and reassure them that you are monitoring the group and have dealt with any rule breakers.

CHAPTER 4

TURN MAPS INTO MOUNTAINS

It was shortly before leaving for the INT when I came across a really exciting advert. Well-known polar explorer Felicity Aston had put together The Women's Euro-Arabian North Pole Expedition 2018. She was looking for ten women from Western and Arabian cultures to join her on an expedition to the North Pole. Team members would be involved in organizing logistics and sharing their experiences, and all costs would be covered by sponsorship from companies. It was a ridiculously exciting opportunity, so of course I applied. It had everything I was looking for. Adventure, connection, and, perhaps most of all, an opportunity to belong to something bigger than myself. It all felt a little, well, special!

Not surprisingly, I didn't get a place; Felicity received over 1,000 applications!

It's never nice getting a rejection email and, of course, I was disappointed. I'd started to daydream about how great it'd be to get a place on the team. I didn't have to dwell long on that disappointment though. The wonderful thing about spending so much time hiking in the desert is it gives you a lot of time to think: time filled with endorphins and, in turn, lots of positive thinking. With all those dusty miles to pass, ideas began to form. I already knew I wanted to launch a group for women who liked the outdoors, but could I be even more ambitious than that? If I wanted to be part of an exciting team adventure—couldn't I just create one myself?

As the Negev mountains were passed, a plan began to formulate for what I would call the Everest Adventure.

Alongside the launch of the new Love Her Wild Facebook group, I also wrote a blog inviting women to join me on the Everest Adventure. Over five days, a team of women would come together to attempt to climb the height of Everest in the Lake District, UK. It was an adventure I'd fabricated. Something that could be achieved locally, wouldn't take a huge amount of planning, and would (or so I hoped) be achievable. We would carry all our own gear; wild camping along the way. Just like Felicity Ashton, I was offering a unique opportunity. Sure—it wasn't the North Pole—but it was still an unknown adventure. Just like the Enduro expedition, the team would be involved in decision-making and planning.

The Everest Adventure blog was shared dozens of times causing an instant rush of new members and activity in the group. I was anxious about how it would be perceived, mostly worried that others would see me as too inexperienced. As is a common theme in my journey my worries were unfounded, and I was soon looking at one hundred applications trying to work out how I'd reduce that down to a final team of nine (me included).

The chosen women represented different ages, backgrounds, and experiences with just one shared focus: the expedition really meant something to them all. The women had been through big life changes or were going through personal struggles.

I don't think I've ever felt so much of a fraud as I did on day one of the adventure. This was my first attempt at organizing a team expedition and bringing together members from my shiny new community. Internally I felt like I was out of my depth, I had done a leading qualification and had all my insurance in place but was sure that everyone would notice that I wasn't a "real" adventurer or community leader. (I was surprised to find out later on that most of the team believed the community had been established for a long time and that leading teams was something I did regularly. Not because of any attempts on my part to hide these facts, but simply because they just took what they saw as face value and didn't care enough to ask. It's worth bearing this in mind if you are worried that others might question your credentials!)

I could have started out with something small. Like a hike or a meet-up in a pub, but instead I'd gone for a big multi-day adventure. With some well-known sponsors—Columbia, TentMeals, and Vivo Life (the women loved the free gear!)— magazines asking to share our story, and now hundreds of women in the Love Her Wild community all watching from the sidelines wondering how we would get on. The buildup and logistics had all exceeded expectations, but it hadn't all gone smoothly. The team all met together for a training and planning weekend—the only time we'd meet before doing the final expedition. Shortly after, I had to deal with what continues to be one of the biggest frustrations that comes with event organizing and planning. A team member pulled out. Then another and another. Three in quick succession. It felt like the expedition was falling apart.

There was no doubt that I took the dropouts too personally, and I was also angry. It was too late now to find replacements from all the women who had applied that I had let down initially. I hadn't foreseen this problem happening; otherwise, I would have had some teammates on reserve. I had no choice but to run the expedition with the five remaining women.

On the second day of the Everest Adventure, I pulled myself out of my warm sleeping bag to brace the cold dew outside in search of a stove and a tea bag. I took in the view around me. Three tents were pitched in a circle and, in the middle, my five teammates all sorting their kits, making breakfast, and chatting with ease. I could already see that the team dynamics had shifted a little. The first day had been long and tough, damp and awkward. This morning though, there was lots of banter and already a familiarity forming with each other.

It was only a few hours into day two of the adventure that I came to the realization that we were going to fail in our efforts to reach the height of Everest. I'd massively underestimated the pace of the team and the impact of the weather and carrying heavy bags. This was made worse when one of the team members injured her leg. As I plodded along at the back, letting some of the other teammates navigate the way, I worried about how they were going to take this news. Or worse, what would the reception be on the outside world. This was my first attempt at organizing an adventure; we'd had three teammates drop out, and now here we were—already failing our goal and not even halfway in.

I waited until we returned to camp and called a team meeting. All of us squeezed into a two-man tent with hot drinks and snacks in hand. By now the team had also worked out the inevitable. Despite the disappointment though, the general feedback was positive. "We were here for a team adventure, not to reach a goal," I was reminded. "We can still carry on and just focus on having a good time, which is what it was all about" another piped in.

So that's exactly what we did.

We made peace with not seeing the peaks of Everest and instead set out to climb as high as we could manage (6,144 meters in the end—the height of Denali) while having a good time along the way. We laughed a lot and chatted nonstop. And over those few magical days, I saw the incredible formation of a supportive team forming a bond that was like nothing else I'd ever experienced.

Amazingly, the reception we had on completion was only one of positivity. Many followers commented how much more relatable we were by not succeeding and how refreshing it was to see a team focus on fun rather than a goal. We even had our feature in the magazine still, instead focusing on how we all overcame our personal Everests regardless of our end result.

It was an incredible experience and I left with a group of friends who still remain a tight team today. The Everest Adventure was the fusing of the Love Her Wild community, and with it, our ethos was set…fun and supportive friendships over end goals—always!

WHAT DOES YOUR MOUNTAIN LOOK LIKE?

Although the hub of your community will be online, nothing will bring your tribe together more than in-person events and experiences. After all, looking at a mountain on a map will never compare to seeing it for real!

The in-person events your group organizes will depend greatly on your community purpose and the needs and interests of your members. They could take the form of:

- Talk nights (a series of speakers from within the community sharing their stories)
- Social meetups (for drinks, picnics, pub quizzes, and so on)
- Going on walks or doing activities together
- Competitions and championships
- Skill building events
- Participating as a team in challenges or sports events
- Campouts or get-aways
- Conferences and exhibitions

If your community is spread geographically, it might make sense to focus your get-togethers in the form of larger annual events. Each year, for example, I organize what I call Wild Weekends. These mini-festivals usually have around seventy women attending. In the day, there are bushcraft sessions, wellness activities, and workshops all on the theme of outdoors and adventure. In the evening, there are inspirational talks, adventure tales, and the occasional game. As well as being hugely popular, and always selling out, they are a great way to bring Wilder members together regularly so they feel that connection to the community and to others within it. We now host a number of these Wild Weekends each year across the country.

Another option, if the logistics of doing in-person events are too difficult, is to organize online events. While it won't be quite the same, they can still serve a purpose in creating community memories and connections. I've seen this work well as a coffee chat (everyone brings a hot drink, and you ask a few questions to get the conversation rolling, maybe using breakout sessions if it's a large group), skill-sharing workshops, or inspirational talks.

CHALLENGES THAT COME WITH ORGANIZING EVENTS

Organizing events is hard. It takes time to plan and sort logistics and maybe even more time to then publicize and fill spaces. On top of that, it's also emotionally challenging. Nerves building up to event day are very common. You might worry that you've forgotten something important. That something will go wrong on the day. The attendees won't have a good time. Or, perhaps the worst fear of all, that no one will show up!

Like with anything, in time organizing events gets easier. The planning becomes less stressful and the worries about how it will turn out will reduce. I've organized lots of meet-ups and events where no one has signed up, or I've had so many dropouts that it's ended up just me and one other person. At the time it can feel like a failure, and I'd get that horrible feeling of not being liked—the same feeling you get as a child when you think nobody wants to come to your birthday party. In hindsight though, I can see them all as learning opportunities. I was discovering what days and times worked better for my community members. What sort of activities really got them excited. I realized I wasn't plugging the events enough—making sure that every member had seen it was running and had been sent a reminder. Free events would always see my highest dropout rates so I try to add a fee, even if just a token amount, to mitigate this.

I built resilience to the enviable dropouts that would come from organizing events. You always get them (10 percent is often considered as a good ballpark dropout rate for paid activities; free events are more likely to be at the 30 percent mark, and free online events even as high as 50 percent...and remember, these are just averages!). It makes it much easier if you anticipate this happening and write this into your planning. It's then just a bonus if everyone does show up.

The nerves about things going wrong also melted away over time. I've organized a walk where I've managed to get the group terribly lost and at a drink meet-up where I messed up the booking. The women showing up never minded, and there was always a solution on hand (Google Maps to help us find our way, and a nearby quieter pub that could squeeze us into a table). Laughing these mistakes off with those who turn up will help break the ice, and you'll soon realize that they don't mind nearly as much as you think they do.

This is also a good time to mention insurance and being a responsible organizer. The legalities on this will change in each country and will be very dependent on what activity you are planning. Before organizing anything, speak to insurers in your field and with other event planners so you know what the legalities are and what good practices you can put in place (such as risk assessments or disclaimers) to make sure you and everyone attending (including yourself!) are protected and safe.

THINKING BIGGER

While regular events and get-togethers serve a great purpose and will likely be a fabric of most online communities (and for many also a source of income, which I cover in Chapter 7), I urge you to also think more ambitiously when it comes to creating offline experiences for your tribe. Could you create a unique opportunity similar to the Everest Adventure?

One of the things I'm often asked by people starting their own online communities is what my biggest bit of advice would be. While growing a community will be a combination of a lot of small steps and a lot of hard work, providing a unique in-person opportunity for my members has been the single most effective thing I've done. It's my golden nugget bit of advice! If done right, I can guarantee this will market your community, attract new members, excite and engage existing members, provide great content, and reenforce your community culture.

There are three key ingredients to make this a winning formula:

1. Provide something unique and valuable

Whatever you organize it needs to be original. Something that will stand out and grab the attention of your members. Think big! What would get you excited if you saw it pop up on your feed? What opportunity would you want so badly to be a part of that you wouldn't be able to get it off your mind? Think about how you can provide value for your members: are they looking for knowledge, to meet an idol, or experience something they can't get elsewhere?

2. Make it a money can't buy opportunity

If instead of the Everest Adventure, I'd offered a free place to hike Snowdon (the highest mountain in Wales), then this would have been nothing more than a simple giveaway. Something that any member could have paid money for to join as tour operators are regularly running this hike. It might have created some interest but nowhere near the same amount. The Everest Adventure was different. It was a team challenge that had never been done before, involving sponsors (who kitted the team out with gear) and press coverage to inspire others.

You don't want to make this a paid-for experience...that's what events are for. This has got to be *unique* and *special* and shouldn't be something your chosen members pay for (this will greatly reduce its accessibility and shareability).

This is where you need to network and reach out to brands and individuals of interest who might be able to provide you with gear, expertise, an experience, or services (ideally free of charge in exchange for exposure in your group).

3. Make it exclusive

You will want to have some kind of application process where you select the member/s based on your pre-determined criteria (this is a great way to monitor that the opportunity reaches your diversity and inclusion policies as well). You want it to feel exciting and an honor to have been chosen. Think about how you can lean into this more—could you write a blog about the chosen members or share a profile on each one of them in your hub?

Creating opportunities with these three key ingredients doesn't need to be a one-off (although you don't want to run them too often or they won't feel quite as "special"—once or twice a year is enough). Since the Everest Adventure I've also offered:

- **The Woods Challenge:** Bringing together ten women for an accessible adventure spending a week surviving in the woods with only basic gear and rations. Bivvy bags and clothes were sponsored by an outdoor brand, and a lady joined us to teach bushcraft skills.
- **First Mountain:** Choosing a team of women who had never climbed a mountain before. Kitted out with sponsored boots, coats, and hats, the team summited Snowdon. A film was made about the expedition which was then shared online.
- **Women's End2End Relay:** I decided it was time to go bigger! I organized a national relay stretching the length of the UK from Land's End to John O'Groats 2,028 km away. Seven hundred women helped carry the baton across 3,000 km in seventy-four days. We had four big sponsors who covered the running costs involved. We posted updates on the relay daily on our platforms. A film was made about the adventure and entered into film festivals. We ran a mini film tour after the relay, and the press covered the story. All proceeds from the relay went to an environmental charity.
- **The Outdoor Academy:** This one was organized by one of Love Her Wild's brilliant volunteers, Sian Brewer. She received grant funding which allowed her to put on a training weekend for beginners in the outdoors covering everything you need to know to get started in the outdoors from packing a bag to navigation. All

accommodation, food, and workshop costs were covered for the fifteen participants.

I appreciate that at this point you might be thinking that all this is irrelevant to you if you are not an outdoor or adventure community. That's definitely not the case though! While adventures are exciting, the core ingredients of my opportunities can be replicated and made relevant to your own tribe. Here's what a unique opportunity might look like for different online communities (note while these will take time to organize, none of them should cost you a penny as you can rely solely on sponsorship from other brands or, as in the case of The Outdoor Academy, perhaps even grant funding):

- **Community for Black fathers**: On Father's Day you want to celebrate five dads in the community who have a special reason for being acknowledged; get your members excited about this by asking them to nominate dads that they think should win. The chosen dads will get a sponsored overnight stay in a nearby glamping site where they will be joined by three wellness public figures who also happen to be Black fathers to deliver a coaching session, a yoga session, and a bushcraft workshop.
- **Cupcake enthusiast community**: Team members are chosen via an application process (they had to share a photo of their most successful cupcake creation yet) to spend half a day in a famous cupcake cafe learning from a chef on how to make their own signature cakes. Cake brands will sponsor the event providing the winners with a personalized apron and utensils, which they

get to keep. The winning cupcake from the day will be available to buy in the cafe for a month, and your members will be encouraged to go and try it out and then share in the group and online what their verdict is.

- **Jewish youth community**: Ten of your members who have an ambition to pursue a creative career will receive an invite to a Shabbat dinner hosted at a Jewish restaurant. Well-known Jewish creatives such as filmmakers, authors, and public figures will be joining to deliver short inspirational talks. Following this, they will share a meal and have an opportunity to network and ask questions. Press from local Jewish papers and magazines will join the event, and the winning individuals are encouraged to create something that represents what they took from the evening; this can be used as content to share with your community.

- **Community for shark enthusiasts**: A handful of lucky members are going to have the opportunity to experience their dream day. They will start with a snorkeling tour to swim with basking sharks, delivered by an eco-shark tour company that has just launched. Later in the day, you will then get an exclusive behind-the-scenes tour at a shark rehabilitation center. Everyone will go home with a handful of books written about sharks. A popular marine conservation podcaster will be joining to produce a special episode on the day and will be interviewing the participants for sound bites.

Now it's your turn. What big ideas can you think up that your members would love?

HOW TO GET A SPONSORSHIP

It's important to remember that a sponsorship is a two-way relationship. You have a very valuable commodity. A focused group of people who all have a very specific interest. For the right brand (a company that wants to target the same audience), this is hugely valuable. Even the smallest companies pay thousands each year to try to reach their target audience. You can help them do this, in exchange for them providing you with sponsorship.

There are two kinds of sponsorships. The first is financial sponsorship. This is when a company provides you with a set amount of funding in exchange for some form of exposure. The second type of sponsorship comes in the form of in-kind sponsorship where a company either provides a product (like a bag, books, food basket, or game console) or a service (like training, hotel stay, haircut, or a meal) in exchange for exposure. This type of sponsorship is usually much easier to get as it costs the company a lot less financially (remember that a product will only be worth the cost price to the company, which is usually much less than the advertised retail price), so it is very low risk for them.

I'm often asked how big your online community needs to be to start getting sponsorship, and my response to this is not very big at all, especially if you are seeking in-kind sponsorship. If companies are smart, they will realize that they are building long-term relationships and that working with engaged online communities is of great value to them. I have been working with a big outdoor retailer since the first year Love Her Wild was formed. That year they provided us with a couple of free bags which we could use as giveaways to just a few hundred in our group. Five years on, they supported us financially, giving five thousand pounds to sponsor a national event run by the community. The group had grown so much that their reach for supporting this was now in the hundreds of thousands. We have a great mutual relationship, which has been benefiting us both.

Asking for sponsorship is really quite simple. It comes down to just that: asking! Here are a few tips to follow to help you secure sponsorship for your community:

- Start by creating a list of all the companies you'd like to approach. You can find them using Google, looking on relevant retailer online shops to see what brands they stock, or even by asking your community what brands they love and would recommend.
- Draft an email to send out to the brands on your list, keep it simple and be very clear about what you are asking.
- In your email, you want to include what the company will gain in return for supporting you (this includes stats such as the size of your group, engagement levels, and if you've had any successes previously such as events that went well or giveaways that were popular). You could offer exposure in your group via your social media platforms or newsletter (adverts, links, photos, and tags). Putting logos on your website or wearing branded gear. A talk from you or one of your community volunteers. If you are working on an event or meet-up, you could offer the company a chance to have a stall or to give a talk.
- When you start sending emails out, keep track of who you've contacted so you don't accidentally send them twice. Use the contact email you can find on their

website unless you have a direct contact or name for the person who is in charge of sponsorships (for a bigger company this will likely be a marketing manager, and for a small company it'll simply be the founder or CEO).

- Send a chase email a week later if you haven't heard back. This is an important step.... I've had more successful responses from a chase email than from my initial contact!

- Don't over-deliver to and under-value your community. It can be easy to offer lots of exposure opportunities, but each of these will take time and energy. Think about the value of what you are asking for versus the value of what you are giving.

- Go in with a higher ask as they can always (and often will) negotiate a lower deal. So, if you are hoping for five books to give to your community, start by asking for ten.

- Don't dwell on rejections. You will get lots! Instead, put your energies into sending as many emails as you can… you'll get a yes eventually. You've just got to keep trying. As your community continues to grow the rejections become fewer and sponsorship becomes easier, especially if you have existing brand partnerships you can contact in the first instance.

CONNECTING PEOPLE IN REAL LIFE

BEN KEENE, CO-FOUNDER OF REBEL BOOK CLUB

The tagline on Ben Keene's website reads "Head in the clouds. Feet on the ground." I think this sums up Ben's achievements perfectly. He's clearly an ideas man who has been involved in numerous groundbreaking projects, but he's also someone who clearly delivers, approaching his endeavors with an entrepreneurial spirit.

In 2006, Ben co-founded Tribewanted, a combination of a global online community that came together to build a sustainable community on a Fijian island alongside the local Indigenous tribe. A project like this had never been attempted before. While there were many challenges along the way, including a fire sweeping through the island, a military coup, and struggles with balancing the online community with the in-person island community, Tribewanted was ultimately a great success.

Ben spent the next years building crowdfunded sustainable-tourism villages in Fiji, Sierra Leone, and Umbria. (If you'd like to find out more about the project, Ben shares his experience in his memoir *Tribe Wanted: My Adventure on Paradise or Bust.*)

Fast-forward to 2015 and Ben found himself living the "cliché digital nomad life in Bali" when he came up with an idea for a new community along with his friend Ben Saul-Garner. They both shared a problem, something which the Japanese called *Tsundoku*—the practice of acquiring reading materials but letting them pile up unread. So, they launched the Rebel Book Club to "share the wonders of reading and inspire a future change-maker."

The concept was simple. They would bring together a community who were interested in reading more non-fiction to inspire their lives, learn about psychology or business, or how to make the world a better place. Each month a book would be selected, and, at the end of the month, the community would have an opportunity to meet in person. From the beginning, members were charged fifteen pounds a month to join (this has remained the same, although now members can also choose discounted annual or virtual membership options, too).

As Rebel Book Club grew, the two Bens experimented with the best channel to host their community online to encourage engagement and discussions in between meet-ups. They've tried Facebook groups, Slack, and Discord, but ultimately settled on a combination of Mighty Networks (who claim to be the only community platform that allows you to run your community and online courses, content, video, events, memberships, and digital subscriptions together in one place, under your brand) and WhatsApp.

As Ben shared in our interview: "It's something we really grapple with. Mighty Networks has all the tools and features we need for online community building. But because members need to log-in or they don't use that app regularly, it's just hard getting them on there and engaged. We get a lot of people filling out their Rebel reader ID initially (on the channel) but then won't keep checking in and engaging.

"Really WhatsApp has driven most of the online conversations. The WhatsApp groups have worked really well and have been highly engaged for a long time. We've got a couple of main ones and then smaller ones for local regions or specific topics that members are interested in. It's spun off in all sorts of directions—there's a 'Rebel Book Brunch,' for example, that's been going on for several years…. That's all been driven by our members."

I asked Ben to expand on his early days growing the community and what he's viewed as key to the success of the group: "The early years of RBC were great. Sunday nights we'd choose a book, message members, set reading goals, and organize a little event at the end-of-the-month meet up.

"We had limited time. It always made some money, but not a huge amount. It was never a big business idea…sure, we wanted it to be sustainable and to have the potential to grow bigger should it get momentum, but foremost it was about inspiring people to read more. So, it was very much a side project—one that we always enjoyed as a team and as a community rather than being on this great big global mission. That's been of great benefit to us, I think.

"In terms of reaching members, it was initially down to word of mouth. We grew from our first fifteen to twenty members in that first month to three to four hundred subscribing monthly members. We got a bit of PR. But it wasn't until 2018 (three years after launching) that I decided to put a bit more time into it. So, two days a week I focused on Rebel Book Club just to see what impact that would have on membership.

"Giving a bit of time to marketing and improving members experience online…. We almost doubled to almost six hundred members a month. That was bringing in coming up to £8–£10,000 a month in subscription revenue."

Seeing that the community was building momentum, the founders decided to launch a crowdfunded campaign to bring in funds for the community. This was a huge success with 299 backers (part members, part friends, and part external backers) pledging a total of £150,000. Following this success, they were set to grow their team and launch a global marketing campaign. Shortly after though, COVID-19 hit and they were forced to change tactics—pivoting to delivering solely digital events.

Aside from the pandemic, Ben shared some of the other challenges that have come with leading the Rebel Book Club: "One of the biggest challenges is how to grow a membership subscription community whilst making it still feel really personal and being connected to all our members. And keeping people on board for a really long time—10–12 percent of members have been with us for three to four years. There's a core group who are fantastic and get a lot from being in the club. Once they've been part of the club for a while, members realize that value—whether it's learning more about themselves, filling learning gaps, building connections, career or business opportunities, reading more, and so on. There are loads of benefits, but it's hard to package that upfront. I think we've always found that difficult."

Another big challenge they face is, ironically, the one they are trying to fix: getting members to actually sit down and read. Departing members often report that they don't have enough time to read the books each month. Steps have been taken to help with this, including sending regular reading prompts during the month—but with increasing distractions in a modern world, this challenge is ongoing.

I've been following Ben via his social media platforms (@ benkeene) for many years and have always found his approach to community building hugely inspiring. The Rebel Book Club is constantly adapting, growing, and trying to increase the value they bring their members. They've diversified the authors they bring on board, regularly offering members talks and questions and answers with their monthly authors. They've recently done a series of events, partnering with Samsung and Audible, and hosted a stage at IdeasFest. Ben shares that they are also looking at how they can provide value to others while also increasing their impact and so are talking to various businesses on how they can play a part in making their team learning and culture more exciting.

It's clear Ben doesn't sit still and is someone who is determined and persistent with achieving his goals. He also recognizes that privilege has played a part in his journey. "I'm increasingly aware over the years of how privileged and lucky I am to have the start in life that I did. I have a supportive family, a good education, none of those structural constraints that lots of marginalized individuals experience. So, I'm glad I've made the best of that to work on projects that have some kind of social or environmental mission.

"The impacts of being part of all those projects on me personally have been largely positive. I've worked with a lot of great people and had a lot of adventures along the way. Of course, I have moments of difficulties. I've got a family to support now, and trying to build regular revenue has been tough in the last few years. But it's a minor stress compared to most. I think the thing I find hardest is juggling different priorities when you are involved in lots of projects. Trying to stay focused and not get distracted. While not spending too much time on the screen—connecting with people and being in person is where the real magic happens.

"I make sure to take care of myself by staying healthy, reading great books and, most importantly, spending time with friends and family."

Ben's three biggest community-building tips:

I keep in mind the three crucial Rs of community building:

- **Ritual**—what makes you a little bit different? This needs to be something that helps you stand out and keeps everyone part of what your community does. Rebel Book Club has a specially designed drink that is inspired by the monthly read and served at the meet-up. Each member also has a say in the monthly vote to decide what the next read will be.

- **Rhythm**—what are you doing regularly that gives your members confidence with what's going on? Rebel Book Club members know that every Monday they'll get a little update newsletter from HQ and that the last Tuesday of every month is an event. In between, they receive reading prompts and nudges. When you build a rhythm that your community members are aware of, it builds trust.

- **Respect**—How will you foster respect amongst your members? This is perhaps the hardest to build. Rebel Book Club has been easier in some ways to build this as we aren't dealing with difficult topics or tough emotions.

We've still had times though when arguments have broken out. We don't have a lot of rules, but guidelines and culture can create a space where members are respected.

Find out more about Rebel Book Club:
rebelbook.club
@rebelbookclub

CHAPTER 5

REACH YOUR SUMMIT

There's a term endurance athletes use known as "hitting the wall." It's when you are hit with sudden fatigue and loss of energy. Your body is screaming at you to stop, and you need to tap into your mental strength to power yourself onward.

You get something similar when you do long-distance adventures like hiking 1,000 km trails. Only my versions were never anything as hardy a smashing through brick walls. My moments of fatigue and exhaustion were usually accompanied by collapsing to the floor and sobbing like a small child. Ugly episodes paired with a lot of uncontrollable snot.

I remember one of these particular moments while hiking on a scorcher of a day in the desert. I had been walking for a few hours by myself and had been feeling fairly positive. My headphones were in as I was listening to a podcast to distract me from my aching legs and the beating sun on my head. From nowhere, my body decided it had had enough. The miles ahead looked like too much and the pack on my back was too heavy.

I willed my legs to keep moving. Don't stop. Keep putting one leg in front of the other. I was so tired. More than anything, I just wanted to stop and for this to be over.

Unclipping my bag I let it fall to the ground, and then the tears streamed down my dust-covered face as I got all the frustrations out.

Eventually, the tears slowed, and I was able to take a few deep breaths before picking myself up and continuing on. It was hard, really hard. Tiring and exhausting. I'd never before been so reliant on myself for discipline and motivation. But there was no way I was quitting, not now after all the work I'd put into getting this far. I wanted to finish this hike more than anything and nothing could stop me.

I carried that same resilience with me on my journey growing Love Her Wild. Because, boy, I can tell you, you are going to need some!

Having leadership capabilities is one thing, but having the confidence and drive to use them is an altogether different battle. It's something many of the leaders in my interviews talked about, such as Mary DeBoise, founder of the Black Girls Craft: "I think I was born with leadership capabilities but fear of a lack of confidence has been a hindrance in allowing me to use that trait to my full potential."

The American author and entrepreneur Jim Rohn once said, "The challenge of leadership is to be strong, but not rude; be kind, but not weak; be bold, but not bully; be thoughtful, but not lazy; be humble, but not timid; be proud, but not arrogant; have humor, but without folly." I like this quote because I think it sums up the ridiculous expectations that come with being the person in charge. You've got to be many things at once.

While you might have been born with leadership qualities, being a good leader who can reach their peak only comes from years of practice and, most importantly, working on yourself. We all have self-limiting beliefs. These are assumptions we have about ourselves and the way the world works. They usually stem from our early experiences and end up holding us back and greatly reducing our potential. Running a community is like opening yourself up bare for all to see, leaving you vulnerable and exposed. All eyes are on you, all decisions falling on your shoulders. You are chasing a dream creating something that is brave and daring. Your self-limiting beliefs are going to have an absolute field day!

I've already shared some of my personal self-limiting beliefs including feeling not good enough or worried that I'm not likeable. When thinking back to my school years when I was bullied and didn't do well in my classes, it's not surprising that this was a narrative I kept telling myself. Of course, neither of these things are true but once set, self-limiting beliefs are hard to crack. They have held me back for years and take constant work to keep them at bay so they aren't clouding my decisions or ability to live my life to the fullest.

You might think this isn't relevant to you, but that simply isn't true. In case you didn't take note of the above, I'll repeat it. We *all* have self-limiting beliefs. Do you know what yours are?

You often hear people talking about the fear of failure, but it's the fear of success that I actually think is holding most back. I found success as daunting and real as any anxiety around my pursuits amounting to nothing. It was when things started to go well that I began doubting my worth and abilities much more than when things weren't going to plan. Surely this was a fluke?

Surely I can't maintain this level of success? Was I capable of having all my wildest dreams come true? Was I worthy?

American author Marianne Williamson captured this beautifully when she wrote, "Our deepest fear is not that we are inadequate. Our deepest fear is that we are powerful beyond measure. It is our light, not our darkness that most frightens us. We ask ourselves, 'Who am I to be brilliant, gorgeous, talented, fabulous?' Actually, who are you not to be? You are a child of God. Your playing small does not serve the world. There is nothing enlightened about shrinking so that other people won't feel insecure around you. We are all meant to shine, as children do. We were born to make manifest the glory of God that is within us. It's not just in some of us; it's in everyone. And as we let our own light shine, we unconsciously give other people permission to do the same. As we are liberated from our own fear, our presence automatically liberates others."

The more you let fear and your self-limiting beliefs rule you, the more you are going to hold your community back. A positive, proactive, energized community leader equals a positive, proactive, energized community. A negative, doubtful, anxious community leader will feed a negative, doubtful, anxious community. Energy flows and energy transfers.

To others Love Her Wild looked like a great success, and I probably looked like I was having a great time, but it was not the case. I'd been running the community for a couple of years, and I was feeling out of my depth. I'd picked up a terrible habit of comparing myself to others—watching larger communities and public figures closely, fueling the feeling that I was not good enough, and my success so far was nothing more than a fluke. This ritual was eating my time. I was working unhealthy hours. My doubts and fears were spiraling, and I noticed that things in the Love Her Wild group just seemed to be going wrong more than normal. I desperately needed a break and some space to regroup.

It can be hard to take a step back from your community, but sometimes it is the right thing to do. At the time, I was worried that doing this would mean losing everything I had built. Unraveling all the hours and work I'd put into Love Her Wild, but I felt like I didn't have a choice. I took a couple of months off and ignored the messages and admin (other than keeping the bare minimum ticking along). As I expected, engagement dipped considerably in the group. The stream of new members wanting to join came to a halt.

During my time away I did some traveling, going on adventures that weren't for my brand or community but simply for myself to enjoy. I achieved one of my biggest dreams, swimming with humpback whales. It felt so great to not have the pressure of my online community admin constantly there.

After a few weeks, I felt the urge to start reading books by individuals who had been on great personal journeys or were bravely pursuing dreams of their own. I read *Help Me!* by Marianne Power, *Educated* by Tara Westover, and *#Girlboss* by Sophia Amoruso. The book that had the biggest impact though was Brené Brown's *Daring Greatly*. Brown also has a fantastic TED Talk along with a number of other books around the topic of vulnerability. One thing she said that struck a chord is, "Vulnerability is not winning or losing; it's having the courage to show up and be seen when we have no control over the outcome. Vulnerability is not weakness; it's our greatest measure of courage."

It made me realize how the bad habits I had picked up were me masking my vulnerabilities, shying away from my biggest fears, rather than facing them head-on. It was time to step back into my role of community leader with more courage!

The second-best decision I made during that time was taking a break from running Love Her Wild. Space and distance do wonders, and I was able to regain some of the energy and motivation I lost. The best decision I made was starting counseling. I found the process to be exhausting, uncomfortable, upsetting, freeing, liberating, and fascinating all at once. It was counseling that ultimately had the biggest effect on me by challenging my self-limiting beliefs, recognizing my fears, and building the courage to show up and be vulnerable. Thank you Brené Brown (and my counselor!) for getting me there.

When I returned to working on Love Her Wild, things changed greatly. I began working with a great business coach named Charlotte Fowles (you'll hear more from her at the end of the chapter). It was wonderfully refreshing having someone to talk through problems with and to be with me while I navigate making decisions for my online community. I blocked all the accounts that I was checking regularly and using as comparisons to start breaking unhealthy habits. It made me realize how many times I was checking them on autopilot.

Self-care and better working practices became a priority. I created clear working spaces, switching off and having a strict no-screen rule past 8:00 p.m. Running and yoga helped massively. As did introducing a morning routine. Before working or checking my phone, I'd exercise, meditate, and do some journaling at the start of every day.

To my surprise, my work had not been undone by taking a break. In fact, when I returned to Love Her Wild with a gentle relaunch, it seemed like the members also returned with newfound enthusiasm and energy. It took just a few weeks for engagement to go back to where it was before...and then to overtake considerably! We were getting more new member requests than ever, and opportunities were landing in my inbox every week.

I was thriving. And so was Love Her Wild.

CHOOSING TO BE POSITIVE

Working on yourself and tackling your fears should be a priority for reaching your potential as an online community leader. There's another really important part of the process though that I wanted to mention. And that's simply choosing to be positive.

Being positive is a conscious mindset we can choose, and, over time, I can see that this mindset has benefited me greatly. Challenges and problems will undoubtedly come your way. There is nothing wrong with having a cry and acknowledging the emotions that make us feel anger, frustration, or hurt. In fact, noticing these and giving yourself space to feel them is really healthy. What's not healthy is dwelling on them. Ranting, playing the victim, moaning, bitching, and spreading negativity with others is not going to solve the problem; it's going to make you and it worse.

Snap out of it. Positivity is a choice!

Call a friend who you know is upbeat and will cheer you up. Go for a brisk walk or run. Put on your favorite song and dance like a maniac. Meditate for ten minutes. Change the energy in your body and then sit down and look at your problem again, or more specifically how you can reframe it. When you choose to be positive, you will tap into better problem-solving skills, and you'll be more creative. It will feel lighter and take less of your energy. With this mindset, you'll attract the right kind of people you need to support you and see clearly how you can overcome any challenge.

Just recently I had to remind myself to be positive. I had organized two big overseas expeditions: taking a team of ten women to Tanzania to swim with whale sharks while collecting data to contribute to conservation efforts. I was being ambitious running two of these trips back-to-back, but financially it would be a huge boost for Love Her Wild along with the local teams and businesses in Tanzania who benefited greatly from this trip.

I launched the first expedition, and in just a few days sold all the spaces. I launched the second, and over the space of a couple of weeks sold another eight spaces. Then the bookings abruptly stopped. I tried a few more posts advertising the expedition and reached out to some inquiries that hadn't followed through with bookings, but nothing came of them. More posts and stories followed—but nothing. After the initial burst of excitement, it was like watching tumbleweed. This was a disaster. I desperately needed those last spaces to sell to make the expedition viable; currently, I was set to lose money! Those remaining empty spaces haunted me and felt like a huge task. How can I convince women to join? Was the trip too expensive? Had I been too ambitious?

That negative spiral was beginning until I stopped myself short of falling into a dark pit, one that is very deep and can be very hard to crawl out of. This wasn't helping. I made myself a cup of tea and sat on the bench in front of my house and just took ten minutes to be mindful and to breathe in some of the warm summer air. When I returned to my desk, I got out a pen and paper and began scribbling about how I could turn this problem on its head and think more positively about the challenge. I almost laughed out loud because it was ridiculously easy to find. Sure, I had three empty spaces but I also had seventeen booked! Seventeen women who, with barely any notice, had jumped at the opportunity to book onto this expedition. Not just any expedition, a brilliant expedition. I looked back at photos and testimonies of women who'd done this trip before. It had been life-changing for many of them. I'd forgotten how beautiful the island was where the expedition took place, how friendly and fun the locals were, and how extraordinary it was to share this experience with a team of women who I could guarantee by the end would have friends for life.

Suddenly there was no problem in front of me at all. I was excited to find those last women who were lucky enough to experience this expedition, and I *knew* it was simply a case that they simply hadn't heard about it yet. Brimming with enthusiasm, I quickly wrote a newsletter and scheduled some new posts. Knowing that word of mouth is a great marketing tool, I also emailed previous participants to ask if they'd share the trip with their friends.

Within *just two days* the last three spaces had sold. Not only that but the inquiries kept coming, and I now had a huge waiting list. It was clear that the change in tone of the content I was putting out was all that was needed to get the job done. It's no wonder that no one was responding to my content when it had come from a place of stress and worry.

A great reminder that positivity is a choice, and it's a good one to make!

TOOLS FOR REACHING YOUR POTENTIAL

We are all different, so it makes sense that the tools we equip ourselves with as leaders are going to vary. Below is a list of ideas of things you can try and incorporate into your day that will help you challenge your fears and self-limiting beliefs, work efficiently, and ensure you are prioritizing self-care.

Like with any habit change, incorporating these will take time. This is also an ongoing process and something you should keep coming back to. I regularly try different combinations and techniques because something that worked for me last year just might not be as effective now.

- **Exercise**—Exercise can improve muscle strength and endurance, and delivers oxygen and nutrients to our tissues. It supports efficient cardiovascular systems, gives us more energy, reduces stress, and boosts our mood. That's a lot of great benefits to be tapping into! Try to find an exercise that you love doing so that you can incorporate it into your week without it feeling like a huge chore. Be it going for runs on your own with your favorite tunes blaring, a walk on your lunch break, or joining a local team sport.

- **Meditation**—In his book, *Tools of Titans: The Tactics, Routines, and Habits of Billionaires, Icons, and World-Class Performers*, Tim Ferriss interviews more than two hundred of the world's most successful individuals. This included celebrities, athletes, entrepreneurs, and scientists. He found an interesting consistency with all of the individuals he interviewed. More than 80 percent of them practiced some form of daily meditation. This is not surprising when looking at the huge number of benefits that meditation can give you including increased focus, reduced stress and anxiety, and enhanced moods. There are many different types of meditation you can try from Transcendental, Mindfulness, or Movement. You can try using an app for guidance or simply setting an alarm and following your chosen technique for ten or fifteen minutes a day.

- **Breathwork and cold-water immersion**—There are a lot of alternative practices that claim to relax the nervous system, increase concentration, improve well-being, and circulation. Breathwork and cold-water immersion are two practices that are both greatly increasing in popularity. Much of this movement has been led by the extreme athlete and motivational speaker Wim Hof (also known as The Iceman). Wim claims that "if we always choose comfort, we never learn the deepest capabilities of our mind or body." Through his books, talks, courses, and app, he leads breathwork sessions and daily cold showers. As someone who now practices both of these regularly and can see huge benefits with my work, I can highly recommend giving them both a try.

- **Healthy eating habits**—What we eat has a huge effect on our health, energy, and mood level. Think about your diet and eating habits to look for changes you can make to ensure you are working at your best. You could try following a food plan or speaking with a dietician if you think you'd find this beneficial.

- **Therapy**—There are many different types of therapies including psychoanalysis, behavior, cognitive, humanist, and holistic. They all involve meeting with a therapist to resolve problematic feelings, beliefs, relationships, and behaviors. The stigma around therapy is shifting and we are starting to realize how counseling can benefit all of us, as no one is saved from traumas and beliefs carried forward from their past. Working with a counselor may benefit you greatly as a community leader so that you can better understand yourself and free yourself from thinking that may be holding you back.

- **Routines**—Developing routines could help you work effectively and in a way that is balanced and conscious. Like me, you might like to craft a personalized morning routine that could include anything that you find beneficial such as exercise, meditation, or journaling. Similarly, an end-of-day routine could help you switch off and maintain a healthy work/life balance. You might end the day by writing your to-do list for the next day or packing away your desk and laptop to signal that work is done for the day.

- **Mentor**—Having a mentor, someone who you can lean on and learn from, could be a great support on your community leader journey. Usually, a mentor will be someone senior or someone you admire who is further along on in their career than you and who you meet or speak with regularly. If you think you'd benefit from a mentor, make a list of individuals who you think you could learn from. Make contact with them and ask if this is something they'd consider doing. Ensure you have laid out guidelines (for example, you don't contact them between your meetings) so it's clear you won't become a burden or use too much of their time. It can be an honor being asked to be someone's mentor, and, if they also received help getting to where they are, a nice way for them to repay the favor. So don't be shy to ask.

- **Reading**—You might want to simply use reading as a way to relax and carve self-care into your routine. Reading can also be a great source of information, inspiration, and knowledge, be it reading books from other community leaders sharing their stories or ideas from successful entrepreneurs.

- **Coaching**—A qualified business or life coach will be able to support you in achieving specific goals by providing training and guidance. Usually, coaching takes the form of regular, in-person, or online sessions lasting an hour. Being an online community leader can be an isolating role, so having a coach can be hugely helpful when it comes to tackling problems and being clear about your direction and outcomes.

- **Support groups**—Do an online search or ask business owners in your area if they know of any support groups for entrepreneurs. These spaces are usually there to network and share with others who can relate to your struggles. Joining support groups has led me to find new supportive friends, collaborations, winning awards, and even receive funding. As a community leader you might feel a bit strange joining a group aimed at business owners, but running a community comes with the same challenges as growing any organization, so my advice is to own the term "entrepreneur" and get networking.

- **Do things that scare you**—I couldn't agree more with Arianna Huffington, cofounder of the *Huffington Post*, founder of Thrive Global, and author of fifteen books when she took to Twitter to say, "Fearlessness is like a muscle. I know from my own life that the more I exercise it the more natural it becomes to not let my fears run me."

Getting comfortable with doing things that scare you will help you greatly in your mission to build an online community because doing so involves lots of bold and scary steps. It's no coincidence that I launched Love Her Wild right after I had finished my long-distance hike. An adventure that forced me to face my fears and bravely try new things out of my comfort zone. I now regularly try to exercise my "fear muscle." Through work—sending out bold emails or asking for money as a speaker—or in my personal life—trying a new sport or showing up to events alone.

- **Journaling**—Founder of TOMS Shoes, Blake Mycoskie, often credits much of his success as an entrepreneur to a habit he began as a teenager: journaling. He journals every day, using the exercise to work through worries or problems, to clear his mind, and set new goals. There is no right or wrong way to journal, but this simple habit could be a great tool to incorporate into your day.

- **Affirmations**—Affirmations involve repeating positive phrases to yourself (often reframing negative thoughts you consistently have) on a daily basis. Self-help books regularly promote affirmations, and there is also some science to back their ability to change mood and productivity.

QUICK TOOLS FOR WHEN YOU'RE FEELING OVERWHELMED

Being a community leader equates to having to make a lot of decisions. On some days, I feel the pressure of all the thousands of members on my shoulders. On those days, it can take something really small to tip my mood—a rejection email, an overspilling email, or someone canceling on an event. Suddenly I'm feeling stressed and anxious.

While the tips above are focused on taking on board bigger daily habits and lifestyle choices, sometimes you need a quick fix in the moment. Here are some techniques I've picked up along the way:

- **Breath**: Try taking a few deep belly breaths, making the exhale longer than the inhale. Or try box breathing for a few minutes (in for four, hold for four, out for four, hold for four, and repeat).
- **Allow yourself to think worst-case scenario**: Often it is fear making us feel overwhelmed. So, spend some time thinking about the worst-case scenarios (no one will show up for the event, your emails will go unanswered, you will get bad press, and so on). For each scenario, really imagine what that will feel like and how you will handle it. Usually there's a simple solution. Sitting with your "worst-case scenarios" for a bit and realizing you are equipped to handle anything that comes your way will make it all feel a bit more manageable.
- **Make a list**: Keeping lists is a really good way to stay organized. Download everything on your mind by creating a huge list of tasks that need to be done. Then order them in terms of priority—what needs to happen now, what can wait until next week, and what can wait

until a later date. Just focus on what needs to be done now and, as much as possible, start with the biggest most daunting task. Getting this ticked off first will make the rest look easy.

— **Use the five-second rule**: If you are still struggling to get your tasks done, I'd suggest checking out Mel Robins and her "Five-Second Rule" concept. It's a countdown tool you use (literally saying to yourself "five, four, three, two, one") when you are procrastinating or getting distracted. It really works, and before you know it, you'll be clearing your to-do list like a pro.

— **Shake up your mood**: Quite literally. Get up and jump around, go for a brisk walk around the block, or play your favorite song at full blast and dance like it's the last song you'll ever hear. It works!

TAKING A BREAK

There might come a time when you feel it's right for you to take a break from your role. Many of the leaders I interviewed in this book had taken time away from their groups at some point, like Hannah from Speak Your Truth who took six months to allow herself time to deal with personal challenges before turning her attention back to her group. When I asked Wes from Solo Armada what the biggest challenge of managing a community is his reply was, "Burnout. Pure and simple!" His advice to others is to know when to leave it alone: "Do your [day] job. Spend time with a loved one. Chill out and then sleep. You need to recharge and the best way to do that is step away completely. I find it really does help as when you do step back in you're really ready for it."

There are different ways you can take a break. You might want to do this in small steps and integrate it into your week, such as taking a day off a week from your phone and emails to focus on self-care. Sometimes though, a bigger step back is needed to reenergize and gain some perspective. Don't be afraid to do this. Your community will still exist when you get back, and, if appropriate, you can find volunteers to step in to help run it while you are away.

If you do decide to take a break from your community, follow these steps to reduce admin, protect the community you've built, and ensure you make the most of your time away:

- If you are able to, appoint trusted members, volunteers, or staff to take over carrying out priority tasks while you are away (such as moderating the group, answering messages, and approving new members).

- Set up automated responses for anything that isn't being monitored (such as emails and Facebook messenger) so any sender knows you are taking a break and won't be expecting a reply.

- Make an announcement in your community explaining that you are taking a break and for how long—inform your members of what they can expect during this time (i.e., do you have new moderators, will the regularly scheduled posts continue, will they stop, etc.).

- Have a clear plan and boundaries of how you will use your time away—is it best to remove apps from your phone so you aren't tempted to check in with the group? Will you be asking step-ins for occasional updates or do you want no contact? What do you hope to get out of this time and how will you achieve that best?

- Create an action plan for your return. There will likely be a lot of workload initially to catch up with messages and admin tasks.

WALKING AWAY

You might also one day have to face the fact that you no longer want to run your community. Inspired by the November Project which kick-started in Boston (november-project.com), Danny Bent founded the Project Awesome community—providing free fitness classes with a difference. In their own words, "We hug. We high five, we behave like overgrown children and get 'accidentally' badass fit in the process."

For three times a week, Danny would run an hour-long fitness class in his hometown of London kicking off at 6:30 a.m. In between the classes, Danny managed his growing community's social media pages and Facebook group, carried out interviews, and chased down opportunities to help grow the community. What started as three people showing up on the first session, grew to sometimes over three hundred braving the early morning class—no matter the weather. They'd always meet for coffee afterwards, something Danny shared in the *Knowing When to Quit* podcast hosted by Sarah Weiler: "The workout would go on for an hour, and we'd always end up going back to a coffee shop…. If you're ever going to do anything like this, whether you're setting up any sort of community, there has to be some sort of external part of it where people get to just go and sit and express their hearts and their desires."

From the outside, you might look at Project Awesome's success and think Danny would be at the heart of it having the time of his life. In the same podcast, Danny shared very honestly his personal battles as Project Awesome grew. He explained that in time, the work he put into running the community was to his detriment, "It slowly took away my energy for myself...by the time I quit doing PA I was probably on the verge of having a breakdown.

"The thing is, I'm sure loads of people can kind of understand this, you've got all these people coming, and this experience is changing their life. And, at that point you think, there's no way I can quit.... [In time it] became clear that I needed to get out of it. For the good of everyone, not just for me. And I just spoke to four of the, kind of, super core members about it, about the fact that I had to go. I thought I'd have to close Project Awesome down because everything was on my shoulders. And they were just like, 'We'll take it on. We'll take it on between the four of us.'"

Danny talked of the relief he experienced first admitting to a friend that he wanted to quit. He compared it to "finding the holy grail" and related it to hearing once that J.K. Rowling, under pressure to write her next *Harry Potter* book, had wished she had a broken arm just so she could have an excuse to step back from it all.

Danny shared in the podcast that once he'd handed back his community, he consciously distanced himself. His own health changed for the better. It was also a time for reflection, "I'm sure I went through a kind of re-evaluating what you stand for, who you are."

Project Awesome continues to be run by "Awesome HQ"— a team of core members. Danny continues to pursue his passion and still grows communities. As well as pursuing adventures and giving talks, he cofounded the World Relay company which has brought over two hundred thousand people together

IT'S TIME TO START CHANGING THE VOICE OF YOUR INNER CRITIC

CHARLOTTE FOWLES, EXECUTIVE COACH AND PUBLIC SPEAKER

While I can share my own experience and the learnings from other community leaders, it felt like this section wouldn't be complete without hearing from an expert on the topic of "reaching your potential." Charlotte Fowles is an executive coach and public speaker who specializes in silencing the inner critic and increasing real self-confidence, real self-belief, and an inner peace and happiness that changes lives. She also happens to be my personal business coach and the person who helped me understand myself better as a community leader, and who led me to making bold changes in the Love Her Wild community—changes that led to tangible success and growth.

In her own words, "I specialize in working with those who feel trapped by their inner critic, who fear they are not good enough, feeling as if this dictates their life and holds them back. I help them to become free from this and to develop deep self-belief, unapologetic confidence, and to believe their own worth, success, and achievements. They often fear being 'found out,' and some may know it as imposter syndrome—but the label isn't important—what matters is they are able to develop their self-trust and live with more purpose, passion, and peace."

Charlotte is also no stranger to overcoming adversity. Her own experience enabled her to go through the same process she works through with clients.

"I endured over a decade of significant personal trauma—which included cancer and a year of chemotherapy, multiple miscarriages and associated operations, suicidal depression, the death of my father, the death of my best friend, an accident that left me with a severely broken leg, and then the breakdown of my marriage. I managed to survive all of these experiences and become an expert in developing resilience, and yet, I was still constantly battling with my 'kryptonite'—my inner critic.

"Having a naturally exuberant personality, people wrongly assumed that this was confidence and self-belief, but the reality couldn't have been further from the truth. My self-confidence was very, very low. Any success that I had was in spite of this inner critic that I struggled with. This internal 'voice' had so many refrains that fueled my limiting beliefs and self-doubts. I never, ever thought I was good enough, no matter what I did. Some of its favorite choruses included:

> You're a failure.
> You are too much.
> You're not enough.
> You are fat.
> You're selfish.
> Who would listen to you?
> Why would anyone listen to you?
> What do you have to offer?
> Why would anyone choose you?

You don't deserve happiness—that is why this is happening to you.

"Thankfully, over the years whilst I was ill or suffering from the tragedies, I worked hard in therapy, which gave me a good grounding in beginning to address and understand some of the fundamental pieces. As I moved into my coaching career, gaining even more of an understanding in the neuroscience and psychology of how we all work—how our minds develop and what happens to create these sort of narratives—became absolutely vital and helped me use all the tools I was training in to bring change to myself and others.

"As an entrepreneur, it was even more essential that I continued to invest time in myself in order for my business to be a success, so I could continue to help others."

I asked Charlotte why it's important for leaders of online communities to work on themselves mentally and to break down self-limiting beliefs. She replied:

"Yourself is pretty much all you have! When you have a community or a business in which you play a leadership role, *you* are one of the most important assets. Without robust wellness in all forms, you risk burn-out, anxiety and achieving what you dreamed but at huge cost to yourself.

"It is also true that the one and only thing that we can ever fully control is how we choose to respond in or to any given situation. Many of us waste a lot of time trying to control other variables, but the truth is, you can't. You can have an element of agency in some situations but not control. Therefore, the wisest and most useful thing to do is focus on yourself—how you usually behave, think, feel, and respond. Getting different results requires different thinking and different actions, and the more chance you give yourself through working on yourself or addressing limiting beliefs, the better.

"Being a leader can be very lonely—so it's essential that *you* learn to back *you*. Because often, it will be left to you to do so. And working on yourself and your beliefs is a very powerful way to do this, actively.

"The key to this work is self-compassion. It is the piece that most people find the hardest. This is not some fluffy concept; this is *real* and powerful. To be able to actively treat yourself and talk to yourself as you would a very dear friend or a seven-year-old child (especially when the inner voice starts repeating your limiting beliefs) is essential. To be kind yet firm with yourself. To understand this basic principle, which I believe with my whole being: that we *all* do the best we can with the skills and resources that we have at the time. If you feel you need more, then learn or get more resources or skills, and avoid shaming yourself for not knowing what you didn't know; not having a crystal ball; not yet being an expert in something; not having the time; not having the energy—the list goes on."

It is old patterns of thinking and old "evidence" that ultimately feed our limiting beliefs. These have been a part of us for years, so it takes time to build on new beliefs. To find evidence that supports our new way of thinking and to train our minds. While this can take months of training and fill many books, Charlotte shared a few techniques that online community leaders can try:

- If a fear or limiting belief comes up, go into research mode...find all evidence contrary to the thing you're afraid of/believing (e.g., others who have done similar things that you've done in the past that might use the same skills; inspirational accounts from others, and the like) and arm yourself with more knowledge or skills to help navigate that.

- Learning to praise and celebrate yourself, is proven to build self-confidence and help with motivation. To treat yourself as you would the most valuable member of your team and you would be heartbroken if you left. As the saying goes: don't wait till you've reached your goal to be proud of yourself. Be proud of every step you take towards reaching that goal.

- Use as many tools as you can to fuel your motivation and belief: vision boards, talking to inspirational people, staying away from negative/fear-based people, learning what you can to boost your confidence in a particular area/skill, and/or getting expert help and advice if needed.

- One of my favorite phrases I heard is "confidence is a result, not a requirement," and there is truth in this. Much of what we do may require some bravery or element of risk to start with in place of confidence of the outcome, and it's amazing how much confidence we can gain by doing. If you're struggling to get going or take that step, ask someone to join you or support you in some way; this is incredibly effective. Few of us can do everything alone, so we may as well get support.

- Do small, incremental versions/steps of what you need to do that build a little more confidence each time—perhaps learning or trying out an element of something new each time and then testing and failing in a safe space.

- For some, building up the steps in stages works. Some people prefer to dive right in, the complete opposite of where they are now and just *go for it* and figure it out on the way. But this doesn't work for everybody or every situation. It's neither better nor worse, just different. Work out which you are.

- Keep an "evidence board" (a powerful tool I use with my clients) of all the ways you do brave things/are brave/adventurous/confident/are the person you want to believe you are to show yourself proof that you have capabilities that you can transfer—and look at that every single day. It's natural to gloss over old achievements once we think they are in the past, but they are still valid and reminding yourself can be very powerful.

- The second important point about evidence is what to avoid doing. For example, if something doesn't work, or you get a rejection from putting yourself out there (perhaps for an opportunity or funding), try not to allow thoughts that go something like this: "Great. Another rejection. That means I'm never going to get published and my idea is clearly crap." Nope! X does not equal Y! This "rejection" isn't evidence of anything other than this particular person or organization not finding this the right match at this particular time. That's it. Being able to counter these thoughts with actual facts helps a lot.

- Know yourself. Know what is a good level for you to operate at. Find your balance that feels right for you, and then stretch yourself a bit—and know when you're tipping into "attempting to control" mode. Be safe in whatever that means for you, be responsible, but you cannot plan for everything, and you cannot control much, so learn how to trust yourself when making decisions.

- Surround yourself with the people who will help boost you, not drain you with their fears or worries. They say that you are the average of the five people that you spend the most time with, so be deliberate with who these are. Sometimes we cannot always manage the five people that are physically closest to us and whom we spend the most time with, but we can supplement virtually; for example, you can listen to podcasts from the sort of people who have a similar drive or vision or are in the same industry as you. Find the people who are balanced enough to help motivate and support you.

- Be careful with information flow. In this world, we need honest, critical friends and mentors who can give constructive and objective thoughts and feedback, so ensure that you are discerning about who they are and keep this circle small. Not many other people's opinions actually matter. They don't. But many people will offer them on your project/idea/community and sometimes can be overwhelmingly negative—even when these are people who love us and mean well. This can kill enthusiasm and provide incorrect "evidence" that your belief system might latch on to. Ensure that you have a few trusted advisors and sounding boards and limit the information you share with others until you need to.

- Avoid shaming yourself for fear or worry. Fear and worry are simply you trying to keep yourself safe. Learn to hear the thoughts and say "thank you for keeping me safe, I've got this/I'll figure it out/get more info/

do more training...." If you try to fight it in defensive mode, the thoughts will dig in, and you're more likely to spiral!

— Finally, *rest*. "Rest day is training day." A rested mind and body are healthy and are proven to make better decisions. It's also a lot easier to manage unhelpful beliefs and thought loops when you're not exhausted. Avoid the scarcity mindset trap that might keep you spinning and working at all hours. Often in this work, we could work twenty-four seven, and it is never done—there's always something more we could do. So, get clear on priorities and boundaries and keep them.

Charlotte makes it clear that your health and taking care of yourself should always take priority. "Take it from someone who has been through more than enough health issues, nothing is worth your health." If you feel yourself reaching your limit or burning out, be proactive in setting up support for yourself and asking for help. "The paradox is that most people love to help and love to be asked for help, and very few of us are good at actually asking."

Her final bit of advice is simply, "If you want different results, you need to do differently.

"If you don't yet do any inner work, start today. Even something as simple as reading a book or listening to a podcast can provide great insights or shifts in thinking. You will be amazed at what a simple exercise can reveal—perhaps a thought loop that you get stuck in, a pattern that you weren't aware that you had because you were too deep in it, and once you see, you can't unsee. And then you can take steps to change anything that you think needs to. The best time to start is now.

"I can guarantee you won't regret it."

Find out more about Charlotte Fowles:

charlottefowles.com

@fowles.charlotte

CHAPTER 6

REDUCE BACKPACK WEIGHT

Since returning from my break, Love Her Wild had really started to flourish. Things were looking good—the group was active and I was working in a more productive and healthier way. I felt like I'd reached a crossroads though and couldn't decide which direction to take the community next.

Our organized trips had always been really popular and I kept wondering if I should scale up this side of the community. This was certainly the advice I received whenever I spoke with business friends or asked for advice when attending entrepreneur events. There was something holding me back though. While it was tempting to chase the money, I knew that doing this would take a huge amount of my time leaving me with less scope to focus on the community and my initiatives (such as organizing free adventure opportunities).

Love Her Wild was turning three, and I was in the mood to celebrate. On a bit of a whim, I decided to organize a birthday party. I found an affordable hostel which I hired out, and then set about putting together a rough schedule of activities. I invited a mix of individuals who had helped shape the Love Her Wild community by being our most active members, running trips, or by giving their time to help with admin. Everyone contributed a little towards food, and I covered the rest (including ordering a rather lavish Love Her Wild cake—it's not a birthday without cake!).

Something amazing happened that weekend. For starters, we all had a lot of fun! I led a few games and activities—things I'd remembered from my early years volunteering at Superweeks Summer Camps. I wasn't sure how everyone would take to being silly and getting competitive—especially as most had never met before—but everyone loved it and threw themselves into the games. To top it off, we had someone come in to deliver a laughter yoga session. An activity that started a bit awkward and ended with a room of thirty grown adults lying on the floor in uncontrollable fits of laughter.

The most valuable part of the weekend for me was running a feedback session. Some of the comments I received I already knew—parts of the website need updating—but some came as a real surprise. Every single breakout group fed back with the same thoughts on what Love Her Wild needed to focus on next: regional groups.

Up to this point, Love Her Wild had mostly existed as a main Facebook group covering the whole of the UK. This posed a problem as we grew in numbers and members became more engaged in the community. The main national hub was fine as a space for asking general questions or sharing your latest adventure, but if you wanted to connect with other women in your area this was almost impossible. I'd tested the waters with a few regional groups but the admin and moderating involved had made it too challenging for me to manage.

At the birthday weekend, the breakout groups also gave me a clear solution to this. They suggested I recruit volunteers to manage the local groups and then—so as not to add to my workload—I bring on someone whose role it is to manage the volunteers. I took the leap and recruited someone to help me run the community.

As soon as I was back home, I did the single greatest thing a community leader can do: I listened to my people!

EXPANDING YOUR TEAM

I'm not someone who finds it easy to ask for help. This hasn't been helped by the fact I'd been let down early on in my process of building my community. Someone who was meant to be helping me didn't pull their weight and, when I raised this with them, in anger they deleted the website and Instagram account I'd been working on for Love Her Wild. It had shocked me that someone could act out so bitterly—and although they apologized—it made it really hard for me to trust others with things like log in details or sensitive information.

The Love Her Wild birthday weekend was a healing experience for me though. There in front of me was a large group who had traveled from across the UK, all of whom had given their time to the community. I often felt like I asked too much of others but, at the feedback session, many of them said they wanted to do more. They were eager to get more involved and brimming with ideas. Who was I to stop them? It was time to get rid of my worries. Not least because Love Her Wild was already too big for one person to manage. With a bigger support team behind me, I'd be able to reach so many more.

The first thing I did was appoint a community manager, someone whose role it would be to oversee the growth of the regional groups and look after the volunteers. Ella Hewton had offered to help with growing the regional groups at the birthday weekend, and I knew she'd be perfect for it. Within just a couple of years in that role (working part-time, just a few hours a week), Ella had launched over thirty regional groups, recruited over sixty volunteers (who we call Local Wilders), and organized our first volunteer training weekend. The local groups went from having a combined total of three thousand members to over twenty-two thousand members. I simply wouldn't have had the motivation, time, and energy to take on this project as much as the community needed it.

Seeing how much value Ella was bringing gave me the confidence to expand further. I brought on board a head moderator, fundraiser, and someone to help oversee expanding our Wild Weekends.

It didn't take me long to build back the trust. I recruited my team well, writing clearly defined job roles and, most importantly, following my gut with who the right person would be for the role. They've all excelled, brought new ideas, and helped spread the mission of Love Her Wild better than I ever could have done staying on my own. It's been my greatest learning curve as a community leader.

As Bailey Richardson said in the *Get Together: How to Build a Community with Your People* book, "Amateurs try to manage a community, but great leaders create more leaders. Nearly every challenge of building a community can be met by asking yourself, 'How do I achieve this by working with my people, not doing it for them?' In other words, approach community-building as progressive acts of collaboration—doing more with others every step of the way."

TEAM WITHIN A TEAM

The success of the birthday weekend encouraged me to do something like this again. We ran a training and development weekend (called Wilder Weekend) which any Love Her Wild volunteer or staff member could attend free of charge. It was a similar setup as before. Everyone stayed in dorm rooms and helped to cook meals which we ate together like one big family. The staff could update everyone on HQ news and updates. We then ran some feedback sessions asking how can we support volunteers better and what ideas did everyone have for the future of Love Her Wild. We had a couple of training workshops. But mostly dedicated time to having fun—orienteering, tai chi, and games. On our final evening, we gathered in the lounge for some talks and our Wild Words ritual.

We arrived as strangers and left a close-knit team.

The cost of running this weekend was in the region of two thousand pounds which is a lot for a small community like mine. The impact was immeasurable though. The enthusiasm from the volunteers following the weekend was incredible. Some applied (and won) grants, which they used to better their local groups and to run events; others collaborated to launch new adventures; some volunteered their time to help update documents and—just like the birthday weekend—there was a wave of enthusiasm from individuals wanting to do more.

So, while it's a lot of money, I have no doubt that the return value exceeds this amount. I also have no doubt that the volunteers would be willing to contribute a bit to the weekend if it wasn't possible for us to cover the costs. While it's preferable to offer it free of charge as a thank you for their time, I think it's better to run it with a ticket price than not at all.

As a result of having Ella managing the volunteers and our Wilder Weekends, the Love Her Wild staff and volunteers have become our very own exclusive community within a community. A team of individuals who have a great time when we come together. It's part of what keeps our volunteers loyal and why new ones join up. They want to be part of that, too.

Feeling supported as a volunteer: RACHEL HEALEY, VOLUNTEER "LOCAL WILDER" FOR LOVE HER WILD

Rachel Healey is one of Love Her Wild's most dedicated and active volunteers. She manages a regional Love Her Wild group in Gloucestershire where she lives. This came about as Rachel had commented in a post in the main group about organizing meet-ups in her area. Spotting her enthusiasm, Ella reached out to her directly to ask if she'd be interested in volunteering; she said yes!

Rachel's role includes moderating the local Facebook group, welcoming new members, and organizing regular free meet-ups and adventures for the women in her area.

While I can share my experience of managing community volunteers, I felt it was important to hear from the other side. I asked Rachel what inspired her to volunteer in the first place:

"I'm not even sure initially—it was very much a spur-of-the-moment thing. But I'm very glad I did! Initially I was worried about following the rules and felt there was perhaps a slight shortage of guidance, but as my confidence has grown, I've come to realize that the freedom is a blessing as it allows each group to be unique and personal to the leaders and members."

Rachel has too many fond memories to highlight what has been her favorite moment. She's organized a number of campouts though and also "introduction to adventurous camping" weekends. Many women who have attended provided feedback afterward that the trip was life-changing. "Having another woman thank you for helping change her life is so rewarding, and I don't think that will ever get old."

Volunteering isn't always easy though. As Rachel explained, "I *love* what I do within the local group, but it is time consuming. So, the first thing is balancing volunteering time with family time and work time. Running a group could easily consume every moment of every day if you let it!

"The second thing is dealing with tensions and conflict online. We've been very lucky to have had very little real conflict so far, and when it has occurred, our members have poured positivity and kindness into the posts concerned whilst tagging the admins so we can step in. I've been blown away by how wonderfully our group members have responded to the few times we've had somebody trying to stir conflict."

When I asked Rachel what has been most helpful, she said there were a few things. The Love Her Wild

Volunteer Handbook (a document that includes the community ethos and mission, job responsibilities—along with tips and advice on how they can do their roles well—put together after the feedback session from the first Wilder Weekend). The Facebook group set up for the volunteers to be able to support each other. The in-person training weekend, which was especially helpful for being able to get to know other Local Wilders, and for making great friends who understand the joys and tribulations of running a local community. And finally, "knowing that Bex or Ella are never far away."

Rachel's three biggest volunteer recruitment tips:

- Don't be afraid to be specific about what help you need. Don't be afraid to be fussy in who you take on to help.
- Think about how you will reward your team members and create a sense of belonging within your team. Even if money is short, you could organize a potluck, BBQ, or a walk together.
- Having members on your team who don't pull their weight is a drain on your resources and energy. You probably wouldn't tolerate somebody not pulling their weight in the workplace. Perhaps we shouldn't when they're a volunteer either?

Find out more about Love Her Wild Gloucestershire: @lhwgloucestershire

GRATITUDE, SUPPORT, AND LISTENING

When working with volunteers you should make gratitude, support, and listening your priorities. If you get these right, you will attract volunteers who stay with you. This is half the battle of managing volunteers as recruiting and training new ones drains a lot of time and resources.

Small acts of gratitude go a long way in reminding your volunteers that their time doesn't go unnoticed. There are many ways you could do this:

- sending a postcard of thanks
- organizing training weekends
- get together for picnics or events
- posting online to thank an individual
- giving volunteers an exclusive badge or patch
- organizing regular catch-ups and Zooms
- running awards and giveaways for volunteers

You should be doing everything you can to make your volunteers' roles are as easy as possible. Ensure you have a handbook or documents easily available with all the information they need to do their job well. Provide training if needed. Make sure they feel comfortable coming to you (or an appointed person) at any time with queries or concerns. As well as running the training weekends, we have quarterly Zoom catch-up calls, and we also set up a Facebook group just for Love Her Wild volunteers so they can get to know each other, share experiences, and lean on each other for advice. This has become a hugely popular space.

Make sure you find that balance between supporting and not being overbearing. I've seen great results from adopting a leading style that is supportive and collaborative, but also quite hands-off. Arden, the founder of Her Travels community, has also had a similar experience: "My volunteers know that I have their back no matter what and that they can come to me if they need help, but other than that, I do my best to hand over the reins to them. It's probably not the most typical management style, but it's the one that works for me. I'm not interested in micromanaging the team. All of Her Adventures, all of it, is built on the work of a beautiful and diverse community. I don't want the work of the team to be my voice, I want it to be our voice. I like to think that approach has helped create the incredible and supportive team we have today."

Finally, you need to be listening to your volunteers. Provide opportunities for them to give you feedback be it at an in-person session, an online form, or a poll. Show them you are listening by implementing changes, especially if the same bits of feedback keep cropping up. This is the single biggest way you can show appreciation to your volunteers for their time.

Investing in your team:
HANNAH HOLLANDER, FOUNDER
OF SPEAK YOUR TRUTH

Hannah and her community Speak Your Truth is a wonderful example of how relying on volunteers can enable you to cope with the challenge of a growing community.

In 2019, Hannah had recently left her husband. Not having any education around abusive relationships, it was only when she had left and started doing research that she realized she'd been in one. She was shocked to find out that one in three women and one in four men will experience some form of domestic violence, and she was angry at the lack of information that existed to support those experiencing this.

She felt compelled to share her story—and in one big brain dump—she wrote on her phone notes her experience and how she was feeling. At the time she didn't intend to share it, but four months later on her birthday she decided to post it and "take her name back" on social media. The post finished:

"I only share this because I wish I knew back then what I know now. And if I can educate one woman on abuse, it will be worth it. After I left, I learned that one in three women will be victims of domestic violence from an intimate partner in their lifetime. *One in three.* Many of whom will stay in these relationships for many years. It's time to start educating our daughters on what abuse actually is.

"If you feel moved (and for my birthday!), I encourage you to donate a couple bucks to a nonprofit in your local community that affects the lives of young women like me whose stories are similar to mine.

"Love y'all so much."

This honest and personal post that shared Hannah's story really spoke to those who read it. Hannah never imagined the impact her vulnerable post would have. Within days it had been shared thousands of times, with hundreds of comments, and many individuals contacting Hannah directly. She remembers telling her mom, "All these people just need to talk to each other and encourage each other!" So, on a whim, she created a private group named Speak Your Truth and edited the original post to include the link to join.

Within two weeks, the post went on to have over 123,000 shares, and the group received over 12,000 members.

Speak Your Truth is now a national (USA), award-winning 501(c)3 nonprofit whose mission is to amplify the voices of victims and survivors of domestic abuse. The group is responsible for helping about three people leave abusive relationships every single week. Having a safe space and access to education and support has been at the heart of the community since it was founded. Speak Your Truth has a Facebook page, Instagram, LinkedIn, Pinterest, and website; although Hannah sees the Facebook group as the main hub of the community, recognizing it fosters a community atmosphere that no other platform can replicate.

When I asked Hannah about the early days of launching her online community she responded, "It was pretty wild in the beginning because we grew so rapidly. In those first two weeks when we gained 12,000 members, we had about fifteen people who reached out to me to offer support in moderating the group. We basically took all the help we could get. We eventually developed a schedule, rules, and rhythms in the group and how we managed it. We developed a volunteer training system and have three tiers to our volunteer group management.

"Over the years, we have fine-tuned our methods. We have invested *a lot* of time to our volunteer team and training. Over 80 percent of the first fifteen people are still with us over three years later, and we have grown to twenty-five volunteers nationwide.

"Investing into our volunteer development has been *vital* to the success of our community. I no longer control anything that happens in our group—I have delegated all tasks to volunteers.

"Since we grew *so* big *so* fast, we haven't had strategies for attracting new members until recently. We were in major survival mode for some time! But now that we have plateaued, we mainly attract members through word of mouth. We are actively working towards becoming an essential resource for domestic violence agencies across the nation and have made connections with some key players like Domestic Shelters, The Hotline, No More, and more. We believe that every time a hotline is called or texted, our support group needs to be recommended. It is SO accessible and welcoming. We are able to offer that much needed emotional support through a survivor's entire journey out of abuse.

"We do several things to encourage engagement now—we have daily themes for posting (i.e., Monday is for Motivation, Friday is for Self-Care, Sunday is for Statistics/Education, and so on). We started to realize that the content shared within our support group can be extremely heavy and depressing. We wanted to encourage a mixture of happier posts, and thus 'celebrating freedom' is one of the four ways we amplify survivor voices."

Hannah's journey might seem like the dream scenario for anyone wanting to grow a community. A single post going viral and launching a community with engagement and numbers that take others years to reach. But leading her community has not been without its challenges and Hannah admits to having many "what the heck am I doing?!" moments: "I am a graphic designer by trade (and still have a full-time day job!) So, becoming the executive director of a budding nonprofit has been quite a learning experience for me. I also often struggle with wondering if I am the best fit for the position I am in—but I continue to push us forward—with hopes that someday I will be able to hire someone with much more experience to take our nonprofit to the next level."

The huge growth of her group in such a short space of time was actually one of her biggest battles as she drowned in the admin that came with looking after members and approving posts in the group. The timing wasn't great as she was in the middle of her divorce and completely exhausted. Hannah made the decision to step away for six months while she underwent trauma therapy.

On returning to her community, which had been managed by a volunteer leadership team she'd put in place, she found decisions had been made that she wasn't happy with. Shortly after, she implemented a restructure and brought new ideas to grow and expand that resulted in conflict in the management team. Hannah now describes this time as a "painful growing experience" one she and the community have now moved on from.

To ensure she continues to be the best community leader she can be, Hannah has invested in counseling and executive coaching for herself that she recognizes has benefited her greatly with professional development. She also keeps a close eye on her stress levels, prioritizing self-care. It's been a long and difficult journey, but Hannah is happy she persevered through the tough times: "I'm proud of myself for continuing in the marathon I didn't realize I'd started when I hit 'share' to my original post."

Hannah's three biggest community-building tips:

- Invest in your team!
- Delegate, delegate, delegate
- Make a very clear mission, vision, and rules for the community.

Find out more about Speak Your Truth:
speakyourtruth.today
@speakyourtruth.today

CHAPTER 7

MONETIZING WITH PURPOSE

I was recently delivering a "building a community" workshop. Afterwards, one of the attendees approached me to ask for advice. She told me she had quit her job to pursue her passion of working for herself as an artist full-time. She'd launched an online community for artists and was attempting to sell her art and art workshops to members.

"It's not working," she told me in frustration. "I can't afford to keep trying and am going to have to go back to being a teacher soon if something doesn't change."

I opened my laptop and had a quick browse on her website and community group. It took me about a minute to understand why it wasn't working. I told her that, although she'd produced a great website and had a brilliant idea that perhaps the best way to make this work would be to return to teaching for a bit.

She seemed taken aback by my suggestion, "But…you said in the workshop we should be brave and take leaps? That's exactly what I did."

She's right. I did say that (and I've repeated the same advice in this book). But there's a difference between taking a leap off the side of a mountain into the sea and taking a leap off the side of a mountain toward a rocky path below. You definitely don't want to do the latter!

When I deliver workshops on community building or growing a personal brand, I always leave monetizing to the last section. Not because it's not important but because you'll greatly increase your chances of monetizing an online community successfully if you first lay down good foundations.

The lady who approached me after the workshop didn't have a community. Sure, she had a few hundred members in her artists group, had a nice website, and good branding. However, the majority of her members weren't active. The magic ingredient that makes a community successful was missing and it was clear to see why: her main focus and goal was simply to make money. When I scrolled through the group page, most of the posts were just her trying to plug art or workshops with little or no response. The community was providing no value for its members, so why would they engage?

Leaving a stable job to run an online community full-time is a huge risk and one that shouldn't be taken without a safety net. Building a community is going to take time. For some this will be a year, for others it will be years. This lady was unhappy in her job as a teacher and had ambition, but instead of quitting her job and putting herself in a situation where money became the biggest driving factor of any decision she could have stayed where she was for a year or two (or at the very least gone part-time). In her evenings and weekends, she could have slowly worked on building her community, connecting with members, putting out helpful content, and slowly growing her profile as a trusted artist. Then, when the time was right and she'd laid down some foundations, she could have taken that leap. With an active community and some years of building her name behind her, it's likely she'd have a much better response to her selling her art and workshops.

There are some exceptions to this rule, and I've found examples (not many, I should note) of online communities that have grown quickly into financially successful businesses. This Mum Runs is one of them. Mel Bound launched the This Mum Runs community after a simple Facebook post asking for a local running buddy resulted in over seventy-five mums turning up for a jog one November evening. Half a year after launching Mel was made redundant so she launched herself into running the community as a full-time job by setting up a clear business model and relying on investments. The This Mum Runs website says, "Mel has created a diverse funding and revenue model that has included crowdfunding, private equity, government grants, brand partnerships and ecommerce, raising more than £2M over the past four years."

Most of the community leaders I came across in my searches have a similar story to my own. They launched their communities as no more than passion projects. Over several years, many then found themselves in a position where they could then begin monetizing. This takes some real patience but also comes with less financial risk and allows you to develop your skills as an entrepreneur over time. As Bill Gates once said, "Patience is a key element of success."

I'm grateful to Love Her Wild for giving me many things. Perhaps the most life-changing for me personally, though, is a sense of purpose and a career that I absolutely love. It wasn't a career that necessarily came easily to me. I'd never even considered that I might be able to set something up myself and be my own boss. Work wasn't always something I got on well with, and I spent many years battling to find something that I enjoyed doing. I'd pursue a new career but soon get bored or frustrated and would be on the lookout for the next job—the one that I hoped would finally be the one I'd love. In the years that followed college, I tried video production, working for a travel company, PA and office management, charity fundraising, and teaching. The commutes and dissatisfaction of those jobs weighed me down in those years and greatly affected my mental health.

That all changed though when I started working on Love Her Wild and my personal brand. My job now is communicating with like-minded people (many of whom I consider friends), organizing meet-ups and adventures (and getting to go on many of them), and inspiring others by delivering talks and writing blogs and books. It's a mix of all the things I love. Being with others, organizing, traveling, adventure, nature, conservation, speaking, and writing. It's exciting and creative, fun, and fulfilling.

Of course, my work comes with lots of mundane tasks too like day-to-day admin (emails and notifications!) and keeping good records of finances. But, for the most part, I enjoy my work so much that I'd do it even if I wasn't being paid.

The work itself and the perks are just part of the reason I'm so grateful for the career I've built for myself. I'm also hugely appreciative of the flexibility it gives me. I get a huge say in the direction of the community and can focus on the areas that give me the most joy (outsourcing anything that I feel the community needs but that I can't give it the right amount of attention). I'm my own boss. Each day, I choose my working hours and location and even spent a few years working remotely as I traveled. I've found this style of working has enabled me to work on a schedule that suits me best (since I'm a morning person) while rewarding me with lots of time to spend on things that are really important to me such as quality time with my daughter and fitting in as much travel and adventure as I can.

Running an online community as a job comes with a lot of uncertainty and responsibility, so it might not be for everyone. You've got to be disciplined and able to motivate yourself to get work done. There are often times of feeling overworked or stressed. For me personally, there is no doubt that the benefits outweigh the struggles, though. I can't imagine doing anything else with my life. I get to spend my days pursuing my interests and chasing things that give me joy. The much-loved entrepreneur Gary Vaynerchuk emphasizes the importance of this in his book *Crushing It!: How Great Entrepreneurs Build Their Business and Influence—and How You Can, Too*: "You're going to go through a time where you're not going to make any money. It's not going to be a week, it's not going to be a month, it's not going to be one year. It's going to be years. And during that time, if you don't love what you do, it's going to be very hard to stick it out. That is something that people don't understand when they hear, 'Follow your passion.' They hear rainbows, unicorns, bullshit. But the truth of it is that it's important, because if you don't enjoy what you're doing, you're going to be that much more likely to quit when shit's hard."

MONETIZING LOVE HER WILD

A few months after launching Love Her Wild, I made my first bit of income. This came in the form of a ticketed event (an evening of adventure speakers) that brought in a few hundred pounds. This all went straight back into the community, covering the costs of the website domain and hosting fees.

Later that same year, I attempted to organize my first paid-for expedition. I did this as a partnership with an adventure company who were already set up to run trips. The tour company organized the adventure, taking all the payments directly, while my responsibility was to fill the spaces and to be there on the expedition to ensure the Love Her Wild ethos was delivered. Love Her Wild took a commission for each booking and—when it sold out in just a couple of weeks—I knew I was providing something that the community wanted.

Over the years that followed, I tried selling different adventures and events—some more successful than others—and slowly made the switch from working in collaboration to organizing and running the trips myself. This took a lot of work and was a scary process, but ultimately gave me much more freedom. It enabled me to deliver better quality adventures that were bespoke, fun, and inclusive.

I also decided to launch a Patreon page. Patreon is a subscription platform that allows members to make monthly or annual payments to support an individual or group. The supporters choose how much to give, and, depending on the price bracket they receive benefits such as a behind-the-scenes newsletter or giveaways. Patreon subscriptions have been slow and steady, but in time have grown to be a significant portion of our annual revenue.

It took a couple of years but Love Her Wild now makes a reliable income via our adventures and Patreon supporters and part of that goes toward paying me a salary as its director. I've tried other streams such as advertising and sponsorship along the way, but these never worked out as well or just didn't feel right for the community space. It was definitely a case of trying lots of things and pursuing the areas that had the most success; your members will guide you towards what provides them with the most value.

While there's a lot to get your head around when monetizing an online community—registering an organization, taxes and paperwork, taking payments, and the like—perhaps the biggest battle you'll face is getting comfortable with the idea of making money. It's something that cropped up lots in the interviews. As Arden from Her Travels shared:

"I'm really uncomfortable with charging our members for things because I really don't want to make this special space about money. But a few of my mentors have been stressing that putting value on the amount of time and research put into resources doesn't take away from the benefit of the community. I'm still working on accepting that!"

American artist Amanda Palmer covers the fear and shame that often surround making money in her book *The Art of Asking: How I Learned to Stop Worrying and Let People Help*:

> "It's hard enough to give fearlessly, and it's
> even harder to receive fearlessly.
> But within that exchange lies the hardest
> thing of all:
> To ask. Without shame.
> And to accept the help that people offer.

Not to force them.
Just to let them."

I also struggled with these same feelings. Is it OK to make money when the primary focus is to help others? Will others think badly of me? Will this take away some of the magic of the community? Am I good enough to make money?

Ultimately, as my Love Her Wild workload increased significantly, I felt I had no choice but to start paying myself if I was to keep up with managing my group. I'd often feel guilty about doing this and nervous to sell things in the group.

Now I view making money very differently. There is no shame in earning a living and charging for things. As with anything in life, it is simply an exchange. If you offer something—and your members see value in it—they will happily choose to make that transaction. I now sell with confidence, and instead of wasting energy on unhelpful thoughts (such as "am I charging too much?" or "am I being too pushy?"), I simply put the offer out there for those to accept if it's right for them. As Palmer says in her book,

"Asking for help with shame says:
You have the power over me.
Asking with condescension says:
I have the power over you.
But asking for help with gratitude says:
We have the power to help each other."

I've also come to realize that, far from being at the detriment of the community, our increased revenue has been of great benefit to our members. Love Her Wild still offers all the same things—it's free of charge to join the group and free of charge to join local walks and meet-ups. With the additional funds though, I've been able to do so much more. It has allowed me to set up grants to fund women to join our adventures who otherwise wouldn't have been able to join and pay for our volunteers to receive training and better support. There's also been scope to slowly grow the Love Her Wild team, bringing on part-time staff to help with the day-to-day running of the community. As a result, we've been able to reach thousands of more women. The impact of that is immeasurable, but there's simply no way I could have got Love Her Wild to where it is today running it by myself for free of charge in my spare time.

BECOMING A NONPROFIT

Depending on the nature of your community, you might want to consider setting yourself up as an official nonprofit. I initially set up Love Her Wild as a limited company, in part because this was the easiest and quickest option for setting up an organization officially. As we grew and more volunteers began getting involved, I felt it was the right move to become a nonprofit so as to protect their time and the energy they were putting into the community. Being a nonprofit means that, apart from receiving a salary for my time, I can't profit personally from the community. Any profits that are left over have to go back into the community to help us reach our objectives and goals.

While this does come with some added paperwork and admin taking this step has also come with some brilliant benefits, such as entering nonprofit awards and, most notably, being eligible for nonprofit funding. This is a new revenue stream that we are exploring that is so far proving to be very successful. I've also seen a rise in our Patreon supports as we can now call their monthly contributions a donation.

DIFFERENT WAYS TO MAKE MONEY FROM AN ONLINE COMMUNITY

Monetizing an online community comes down to one thing—providing value for your members. Enough value that they don't mind parting with their cash.

As each community functions differently, what form this takes will vary greatly. Below is a list of avenues you might like to explore. Almost all the monetizing communities I came across in my research had more than one revenue stream.

Community events

Organizing paid-for events comes with a high workload, but if done well it can be a great source of income for your online community. This could come in the form of regular small events (such as evening talks or socials) or bigger annual events (such as a festival, retreat, game-a-thon, sporting challenge, or conference). The latter is likely to have a much higher return on investment as you'll be reaching a bigger audience. If successful, you can develop a recurring signature event like the Black Girls Craft community which runs an annual Black Girls Craft National Conference and Expo.

Black Girls Craft founder, Mary DeBoise, used to work in finance and ran her community as a side hustle until she got to a point where she was burnt out. "I knew for sure that I had to run my own business, several women on my team have gone on to have amazingly successful businesses and platforms. That's when my entrepreneurial spirit kicked in and I took a real hard look at what the members were saying and what they were asking for and came up with a business plan. It was time to take a leap of faith.

"I feel the conference came about as a need to black women to come together and celebrate our creativity. At the end of the first conference, we were already getting requests for information on next year's conference!"

The Black Girls Craft National Conference and Expo is supported by some of the biggest brands in the craft world. At the two-day event in America, attendees can access live demos, workshops, talks, panels, and shopping, as well as receive exclusive discounts and meet-up opportunities with other members.

Mary's advice for anyone wanting to run their own event is, "Start planning early and establish a realistic budget! I also highly recommend hiring an event planner as there were so many nuances that I didn't fully understand. Reach out to sponsors early on…at least nine to twelve months in advance. I sent potential sponsors a deck that really laid out what the conference was going to be about and how they will benefit.

"Lastly, establish a team that allows *you* to be the guest at your event."

Find out more:
blackgirlscraft.org.

Anyone who organizes events will tell you that running the first one is the hardest. Once you've got a framework in place repeating events reduces workload and, if successful, should become easier to sell as you'll get return customers and good word of mouth. If you don't know what event is right for your members—ask! Do a poll or conduct a survey.

Look for ways that you can reduce the overhead of running the event. Can you call on like-minded organizations to give you a free or reduced-price venue? Are there companies that might be willing to sponsor some of the costs in exchange for exposure at the event?

When it comes to selling, keep posting regularly in your community hub to remind members to buy their tickets. You could run an early-bird discount to encourage initial sales.

If running your first event feels too daunting, the logistics and responsibility too much, you can do what I did initially with Love Her Wild and start with a collaboration event. Find an experienced company with a similar ethos willing to run an event specifically for your community (ideally branded with your community's name). In return for selling spaces, you should receive a commission for each sale. As a ballpark, most of the commission I've worked with previously has been between the 10–25 percent mark depending on the nature and price of the event.

Paid membership

Membership schemes can be a really simple way to generate income from a community. There are two ways you can run a membership. You either allow members to join free of charge but then have an additional paid-for membership option available (usually with extra benefits). Or you can simply choose to be an exclusive community, only available for paying members. The latter might be harder work initially as you need to prove value to members before they've been able to experience it themselves. An optional membership, though, might mean harder work in the long run as you need to keep enticing free members to sign up.

There are a few things you will need to consider:

1. Will membership be a one-off, annual, or monthly payment and how much will you set this at (set it higher than you think!)?
2. What platform will you use to manage payments and members?
3. What benefits will your members receive?

If you don't want to manage the admin of hosting this on your website, there are a number of platforms that exist to support membership schemes such as Ko-Fi or Podia. The most used by the community leaders I reached out to (myself included) is Patreon. Although intended for creatives to allow them to run a subscription service for their fans, it also works well in managing online community memberships. You have the flexibility to create different levels of rewards depending on how much members pay and can communicate and put out content directly to your Patreons. Helen, founder of Journal with Purpose, explains why she chose Patreon as a platform:

"I really wanted a safe place where I could offer my community a lot more content, tutorials and printables. Patreon is a well-known platform in the journaling and creative field, so already somewhere that my community would trust. I offer monthly journal prompts, creative challenges, tutorials, lots of videos, journal digital printables, behind the scenes updates and lots more photos from inside my journals."

It can be tempting to try and entice members to join with lots of exciting benefits, but a few done well is better than a lot that are without thought or care. For any benefit you offer, think about the time and money you put into producing that versus the reward you receive back. Ideas for benefits you might like to provide members include:

- merchandise such as T-shirts, posters, or badges
- an exclusive badge or patch
- membership certificate
- behind-the-scenes updates or a newsletter just for paying members
- exclusive content such as podcasts, blogs, or videos
- early bookings for events
- discount codes for relevant brands or money off community events

If you launch paid membership you are going to want to advertise this across all your channels and platforms. This won't be a one-off. Mention it at every opportunity you get be it at the end of your email signature or at the bottom of any community update you put out.

Getting the first few members to sign up will be the hardest (remember, numbers feed numbers!), so consider running an incentive early on such as a bonus reward for any sign-up before a certain date.

Produce content

If you have a clear topic that enables you to produce helpful content, you may be able to turn this into revenue. Content creation can come in the form of video (YouTube being the most popular), podcasts, or blogs.

Making money through content usually takes a lot of time and requires consistent updating. You'll need a good understanding of the algorithms of the platform you use, as well, as

Search Engine Optimization to better your chances of increasing traffic (people viewing your content). Once you've got a good amount of traffic you can then start thinking about generating revenue. This could be through advertisement (such as a drink brand paying for you to give them a mention in your video), affiliate links (you getting a percentage of a product you recommend on your blog if a reader makes a purchase), or sponsorship (a brand paying to be the sponsor of your next podcast).

Having an online community serves this form of content creation well as you'll be able to advertise any new content to your members, which will keep your traffic numbers high.

It can also be used to advertise the community and find new members. If you produce a podcast, for example, then you can mention the community at the end of each episode and encourage new listeners to join.

You could also consider book writing. It's quite difficult to earn significant sums of money from book writing—but it can provide a small, passive income in time—especially if you produce a number of books. For a community, this can work well as a collaboration such as sharing advice or stories from within your group.

Self-publishing has made it easy and accessible for anyone to publish a book. You might also want to try a traditional publishing route if you think you have a good (or more importantly, commercial) idea. While you won't take as much in sales, the finished book is likely to be better with the input of editors and an experienced publishing team. You might receive an advance and, in addition, a published book might help raise the profile and prestige of you and/or your community.

Sell merchandise or a product

Merchandise could provide a great, steady income for your community while also potentially providing some free advertising (great if you can get lots of members proudly wearing your community logo T-shirt day to day!). Merchandise could come in the form of clothing, drink's bottles, bags, wall art, souvenir items following events, or specialized equipment. It's got to be something your members would use, for example, if you are a Warhammer 40,000 enthusiast group you could produce a branded carry case that your members can use for their models.

There are numerous print-on-demand merchandise companies now available such as Shopify or Teemill. Although profit margins are smaller, this greatly reduces workload and means you don't have to take the risk of ordering large amounts of stock that you aren't sure will sell.

You might also have an idea for a product that works well for your community. Claire Russell launched playHOORAY! to support and inspire an online community of parents and caretakers to play with their babies and young children at home. Claire has created a host of resources for her community offering online courses, coaching, regular play ideas on her social media channels, a published book, as well as supportive Facebook groups.

One of her most successful ventures, though, has been launching PlayPROMPTS. These packs of cards include dozens of ideas for play to keep children five and under entertained. As well as age-specific prompts, you can also find a range for eating out, journeys, and outdoor play. PlayPROMTS are regularly promoted in the playHOORAY! community but can also be found on e-commerce websites such as Not On The High Street and Etsy and in stores.

Sell your expertise

As your community grows, the increased knowledge and exposure around your shared interest will put you in a great position to share your expertise. This might be offering coaching and mentoring, writing online courses, or running workshops. Think about who you are targeting. Will it be for your community members or others outside your community who want to learn from you? For example, if you run an online community for Instagram influencers, companies might be really interested in having you deliver workshops on how best to work with influencers. Or perhaps you think you can provide a great online course for individuals who want to be an Instagram influencer and hope to one day be in your group.

Eb Gargano who founded the Productive Blogging Community has made a great success from selling online blog courses. Within three years of launching her food blog (Easy Peasy Foodie), Eb was earning a decent wage. Wanting to give back to the blogging community and diversify her revenue streams, she then launched Productive Blogging which consists of a free website full of resources, a Facebook group, and a weekly newsletter. Alongside this, members can pay for ebooks and courses that also earns them a place in the exclusive students-only community called the Productive Blogging Inner Circle.

Eb initially thought about writing an ebook on productivity but first, she did what she advices all her students to do—ask her audience what they want! (This is something that she learned from having a degree in business and years of experience working in business and marketing.) A clear answer came back: a course on Search Engine Optimization and how to grow traffic to a site. So, using the platform Teachable, that's what Eb created:

"This is a really good example of how what you *think* your community will want isn't necessarily what your community really wants—you never truly know until you ask them!

"It has been far more successful than I could have ever imagined—with some incredible testimonials and success stories from my students. I've since gone on to launch more courses on how to start a profitable blog, how to do email marketing successfully, how to create and launch an online course and how to build an evergreen sales funnel...but SEO Jumpstart still remains my most popular course."

Eb uses a lot of savvy marketing strategies such as running social media ads and using "top of the funnel" freebies. She also advertises her courses regularly in her community, but makes sure to keep a balance with this. "I am careful not to be too pushy or 'promotional' in my community as I want people to feel like the Productive Blogging Community is primarily a community...not a place for me to hard sell my courses.

"My number one top tip is to listen to your community! What are they saying? What are their main struggles/challenges/ problems? What do they keep asking for help with? Then create a course that solves *one* of those problems. (Don't try and solve all their problems in one product—as a general rule one highly targeted product will sell much better than one which tries to do a little bit of everything!)

"Once you have decided on the topic of your course, you can involve your community by asking them what they'd like to see included in the course, what format your course should be (video, text, audio or a mix), what bonuses and printables they'd like to see...and so on. Involving your community is a real win-win: they get the exact course they need, you are likely to make more sales *and*, as an added bonus, it's a great way to get your community interacting with you and each other and for everyone to feel part of the process."

Find out more about Productive Blogging:
productiveblogging.com

Another way to sell your expertise, either as a community leader or collectively with members in your group, is to pitch for talks and article writing. Generally, talks pay much better than writing articles for blogs, magazines, or websites. Think about what your talk could be about and who it is best geared toward: schools, corporates, or events. Put together a speaker's pack and start contacting your target audience. It's a good idea to start by doing a few free talks locally to perfect your talk and to collect some testimonies which you can send out in your pack.

Advertise
Your community is a really valuable asset. In one place, you have collected an engaged group of people who all share a similar demographic or interest. For a brand that is trying to reach the same target audience, this is a very valuable commodity. There are two ways you could provide advertising opportunities. The first is to provide visible exposure for a brand. This could be simply selling an advertising slot on your website, in your newsletter, on your group page (as a post), or as a mention in content videos or podcasts. There are programs such as Google Ads that automatically run adverts on your website but the revenue for this will be considerably less than if you can target a company directly. You might also be able to work with a

brand long-term, providing them with regular exposure on your community as part of an annual partnership.

Another form of advertising is through commission and affiliate links. If you recommend a product to your community and they buy this product or service through the link you share, you will receive a percentage as commission. A lot of brands have affiliate programs already set up, and this often comes in the form of offering a discount code for your members so it benefits both of you. You could have a webpage dedicated to recommended products or brands with affiliate links attached, making it easy for members to buy products while also supporting the community.

There are now regulations in place to ensure that advertisements are visibly labeled, so make sure you are clear on these before posting advertisements on any social media platform or public space.

Seek funding

Most funding opportunities are only going to be relevant if you are a nonprofit. There is a huge wealth of grants available to support community work in all sorts of fields. To find these, do an online search for grant directories that cover your area and country. It's also worth paying your local library a visit often as they can order in a directory of grants for you to use (these tend to be really pricey to buy yourself so using them at the library will save you a lot of money). Grants will vary from small local opportunities for one-off projects to huge funding bids—money that could potentially cover all your overheads for multiple years.

Filling out bids takes a bit of practice, but the most important step is reading the requirements of the funding opportunity and being very clear about how your online community is going to meet the objectives. Doing a survey with your community can be great for providing statistics and quotes that prove you are making a difference.

Grant funding is a numbers game so you should expect lots of rejections. Be organized, keeping track of the grants you are applying for and deadlines. Most tend to be repeating grants, so if you aren't successful, try again in the next round.

There are other forms of funding available for nonprofits including individual donations by running a scheme like Crowdfunding or Kickstarter. This works best if you have a project or clear fundraising goal you are aiming to reach.

You can also look for corporate sponsorship. Most companies allocate some of their annual profits for charitable purposes. While this might just be for philanthropic purposes, it is also a form of advertising as, in return, the nonprofit will usually share the company's logo and publicly announce the partnership. The best approach to finding corporate sponsorship is to use personal contacts and reach out to local businesses or brands that have an ethos in alignment with yours. If you work on building a mutual partnership, corporate sponsorship can result in years of steady income.

If you decided to register your community as a nonprofit organization and pursue funding in this way, it is likely you'll need to rely on multiple revenues. The Speak Your Truth community evolved into a registered charity. Founder, Hannah Hollander, shared that the community is "funded through corporate donations, grants, and crowdfunding campaigns (all *outside* of the support group—our members are the ones who *need* the support, they are not asked to donate.)" This covers the community's overheads and outreach efforts, including paying for three part-time paid staff.

FINDING THE BALANCE

Monetizing your community is a big step. It's going to increase your workload, involving lots of learning and new skills, and will be a journey of discovery as you work out what's best for your people. It's a step that can hugely benefit your members, so keep reminding yourself of this when things get difficult. As Ben Keene (founder of Rebel Book Club) shares, "If you are better at making money, you can provide more value for your community…. If we [Rebel Book Club] had more money now, we'd be doing lots more for our members, whether that's providing more books or running more events. So, I think revenue is really a priority to build on that."

It's important that on the way you don't lose sight of your community's objectives and goals though. You've got to keep a balance. If your safe community space suddenly becomes all about selling, then your members are going to disengage. For this reason, it's vital that you stay in tune to your members and continue to be an active member of your own community. If you keep plugging a workshop and no one is signing up, perhaps it's time to drop the idea and try something else. If instead you launch a conference and it sells out in just a few days, then it's clear you are meeting the needs of your community. If it's a good fit for your community, it should be an easy sell.

BE TRANSPARENT

Above all on your journey to monetizing your community, you should focus on remaining authentic and transparent. Bring your community on board with your monetizing. Tell your members what your plans are and how you intend to make money. As well as how all this will benefit them and the positive changes it could bring your group.

Being honest increases confidence, retains loyalty, and will show you to be a reliable and trustworthy leader. All qualities that will help you on your monetizing mission.

Fabricating a career doing what you love: GAVIN PRETOR-PINNEY, FOUNDER OF THE CLOUD APPRECIATION SOCIETY

I'd never really given clouds much thought until I'd listened to Gavin Pretor-Pinney's TED talk "Cloudy with a Chance of Joy." Gavin crafts his ten-minute TED talk well, using humor, emotion, and anecdotes to captivate the audience. He believes that the sky is the most dynamic, provocative, and poetic aspect of nature. And that spending time looking at clouds is good for you—"good for your mood, your ideas, your creativity, and soul…keep looking up. Live life with your head in the clouds!"

I was excited when I discovered Gavin had turned his interest into a thriving online community—the Cloud Appreciation Society. That, just like me, he had created a career for himself out of thin air. Pursuing something that fascinated him, bringing people together over that shared love. Once well established, he then monetized the community which he now runs full-time. There are not many people who can claim they make a living from sharing their love of clouds…but Gavin is one of them!

Gavin's interest in clouds developed as a combination of his background in both science and art. In 2005, he was asked by a friend who was setting up a literary festival if he would give a talk. At the time, he didn't have a book or website to his name, so he felt he needed to give the talk a weird whimsical name to attract attention. He settled on "The Inaugural Lecture of the Cloud Appreciation

Society"—something he felt he personally would have attended if he'd seen it on a program.

After the talk, audience members approached him asking how they could join the Cloud Appreciation Society. So, on a whim, he set up the community. He built a website (which included a forum), wrote regular newsletters, opened a merchandise shop, and set up a subscription. New members would receive a member's number, badge, and certificate.

For the first ten years, Gavin ran the community as a side hobby and not as a business. The ten-year milestone was an opportunity to reflect, "I asked myself where am I going with this? I was putting all this work into running the society alongside having a young family and a job. I could close it, say 'that had been a fun ten years' or move it to a different place....

"Alongside running the Cloud Appreciation Society, I'd also been giving talks and writing books, some of them bestsellers. This was all great promotion and put me in a really good position. So, I decided to be bold, and I took the step to try and make this my full-time job."

The first step was reevaluating the subscription set up which, at the time, was a one-off payment that only covered the cost of sending out the membership items. Gavin increased the fee and changed it to an annual payment. Existing members had the option to remain members, regardless if they switched to supporting the society with the annual subscription. All new members, though, had to pay annually.

"The big question now, of course, was, what will members get for their subscription? I decided to launch the 'Cloud a Day' daily email which would be sent every morning to members. The email was simple. It has a photo of a cloud, or something relating to a cloud, and then a short bit of text. The photo is often images shared from members (there's a link at the bottom of the email that invites members to submit an image), or could be a detail from a painting or a NASA photograph. There is never any promotion in the daily email. It simply acts to serve our members, to provide them with a moment of reflection."

Over time, Gavin has built an editorial team dotted around the world (who are paid a little but mostly do it for the love of it). Their role is to collect the photos and write the text that Gavin reviews before it is sent to members. This frees up some of Gavin's time. As he points out, "Running a community is hugely time laborious, and I'm always stretched and being pulled in different directions." (Although he does admit that one of his downfalls is wanting to do too much and having too many project ideas!)

Another source of revenue over time has been running trips, such as a six-day tour to Northwest Canada to see the northern lights. The trips include expert talks, tours, and, of course, lots of time to look at the sky! Gavin usually uses a third-party operator who organizes all the logistics, insurance, bookings, and payments. He receives a pre-agreed commission for each booking or works on a system of splitting revenue with the partnering company.

"Although the trips do earn income, they are a different type of revenue. Membership is smooth. It's a steady stream of income. Occasionally the line will start to drop, and I will know I'm doing something wrong. Or it will increase, and I know I'm doing something right.

"Trips though are bumpy—they require a lot of work in advance. You have to sell the spaces. After a successful trip you get a spike in revenue, but then you need to start the process all over again...I can see how they play another important role in bringing the community together. I've loosely tried coordinating local groups with meet-ups with little success so currently, the trips are the only consistent opportunity for community members to meet face-to-face."

Books have also provided income. "I'm reluctant to recommend book writing as usually it's not a good source of revenue. In time though I have made some money from book writing, and it's definitely attracted new members to the Cloud Appreciation Society."

One of his books was translated to Chinese. Gavin believes this is the reason he has seen a surge in members from China. Gavin takes a "Tai Chi" approach to community leading, going with the flow of energy. He believes it's vital that any leader is ready to respond. So, seeing this new energy emerge from China—and noticing a much younger demographic than his usual members—he's looking at ways he can pursue this, including translating the "Cloud a Day" email into Mandarin.

It took about a year for Gavin to reach his goal of making the Cloud Appreciation Society his full-time job. He now has tens of thousands of paying members in over one hundred countries. Members have access to an APP, forums, various social media platforms, and a monthly newsletter alongside the "Cloud a Day."

In that time, he never sought out any advertising but simply relied on word of mouth and press opportunities that came his way. He sees 'being specific and super focused" as being key to his success. This enabled him to raise his profile as a spokesperson for clouds and allowed his community to speak to others around the word. He also mentions the emphasis he put on creating a culture in his community—one that was supportive, inclusive, constructive, and positive. This takes a lot of hard work and moderating but ensures members trust the space and want to be a part of your welcoming tribe. It's this feeling that leads to acts of incredible member loyalty, including a member getting the Cloud Appreciation Society logo and their membership number tattooed on their body, or another being buried with their membership certificate. Another example of incredible displays of trust and loyalty was a 2022 Kickstarter campaign to launch a new website for Cloud Appreciation Day. The Kickstarter received almost double what he hoped to raise following just a single post on their social media platforms and a newsletter (Gavin credits that single newsletter almost entirely for the success of the campaign).

Gavin considers himself very lucky to be in a career that he is passionate about. Like all jobs, it comes with its challenges. He says, "There are many, but technology is my biggest headache," but for the most part he loves what he does. He loves the freedom his work gives him, the like-minded individuals he gets to meet, and the fact that he doesn't need to sit in meetings if he has a spark of a new idea—he can just make it happen.

"I'm sometimes reluctant to use the word passion though—passions are something that are often post-rationalized. For many, the challenge for pursuing a dream career is not how but what or why. My advice would simply be to start doing more of the things you quite like doing. Give yourself the space to explore. Follow what interests and motivates you, what feels right for you. Don't fall into the trap of sitting around trying to find your passion; it won't come. Instead, ask yourself, 'What do I like?' and start pursuing things not because they make you money, it's a good idea or you have a big plan, but simple for its own sake. Simply because you enjoy doing it.

"You will naturally do something well if you enjoy it and care about it. Down the line you can tweak things and start being more entrepreneurial. I fabricated a career out of thin air doing what I love, but it was off the back of ten years pursuing something I enjoyed just for the fun of it.

"There has never been a better time for you to do this. All the tools and mechanics exist and are readily available.

"Don't think too hard about it. Take a leap!"

Gavin's three biggest community-building tips:

- Don't expect to make money for the first few years. Once you've got your head around this, it will shift your thinking and force you to pursue building an online community because you enjoy it—not because you think you have a good idea and will make lots of money

- Collect email addresses from members (it's much harder to collect these later on, so do it from the start). Chasing followings and likes on social media is fickle and exhausting. And ultimately, communicating with your members on social media is out of your control as you are at the mercy of social media algorithms and platforms.

- Think emotionally! Ultimately, it's emotion that drives members to join your community, buy your product, and sign up for your trip. Think about how you communicate. What you represent. What it means for someone to say that they are part of your community and what that feels like to them? What can your community provide that will make them want to be a part of it and tell others about it? This is how you build loyal members who will stick with you.

Find out more about the Cloud Appreciation Society:
cloudappreciationsociety.org
@cloudappreciationsociety

BUILDING AN AUTHENTIC COMMUNITY ALONGSIDE AN EXISTING BUSINESS OR BRAND

So far, this chapter has focused on monetizing *after* an online community has been established. It is possible for this process to happen the other way round. There are many examples of brands who have—either at the time of launching or a later date—successful built authentic online communities. One such example is the Wool& clothing store that set up the Wool& 100 Day Dress Challenge community. Wool& challenges their members to wear one of their dresses for one hundred days straight.

The organization claims online that they were founded on three principles: "live simply, consume carefully, and do good." Their online community and the one hundred-day challenge embodies this ethos. There are many reasons why they encourage members to take on the challenge including minimalism (learning to live with less), environmental benefits (doing less laundry), getting creative with different ways to wear the same outfit, and boosting body positivity (realizing your clothes aren't what defines you).

While the challenge clearly benefits the Wool& company by building trust and increasing sales, this community also clearly provides value to its members. The Wool& 100 Day Dress Challenge community is a safe and friendly online space where members can ask questions and celebrate their experiences taking part in the challenge. If successful with the challenge, members are also gifted one hundred dollars off their next purchase with Wool&.

As the next interview demonstrates for a community to be successfully run by a brand the core purpose of its existence still needs to be to help the members involved; it must go beyond simply benefiting sales. While a brand might have an existing audience eager to join their new community, they are likely to have to work harder to build trust and integrity.

COMMUNITY FIRST, SALES SECOND

....

WENDY RICHARDS, MANAGING DIRECTOR AT THE NAPPY LADY

The Nappy Lady was originally launched to make it easier for parents to choose the best cloth nappies, or diapers, for their circumstances. Rather than focusing on just one style or brand of cloth nappy, the organization provides a wealth of knowledge and represents multiple brands. Wendy Richards came on board as managing director, several years after the organization had been formed.

Wendy decided to launch a Facebook community group alongside the website. "The group was created to give parents interested in using reusable nappies a way to discuss them, get tips but also share their experiences not only of nappies but parenting generally. It also allowed me to directly interact with my customers and support them on their journey." The group continues to support sales for TNL as "parents also share their experiences of nappies and The Nappy Lady, and it gives new parents confidence in the purchase they are considering but also that we'll always be here to help. There is an increasing trend of parents wanting support or advice from other parents, the phrase it takes a village comes to mind, our village is the Facebook group."

As well as having a community group (TNL Parent Group), she also launched a selling page where parents could buy and sell secondhand reusable nappies. Some might consider it strange to have a selling page when the organization is primarily a cloth nappy e-commerce, but Wendy believes that this hasn't been to their detriment and ensures they are meeting their environmental ethos: "we are an environmentally friendly company selling environmentally friendly products so it would be wrong of us to not encourage reusing of nappies. Reduce, reuse, recycle is always the way it should be."

To encourage sales amongst members, products are shared regularly in the group. Members are also awarded a head start on any special sale periods such as Reusable Nappy Week in April and Black Friday in November. These are so successful that sometimes items sell out from group posts alone.

Although The Nappy Lady is a profitable business, the community exists primarily to support parents. Wendy ensures that the company always shares more tips and advice than selling posts in the group. Honesty and integrity are part of the organization's ethos, and, to ensure this is met, ambassadors have been appointed to bridge the gap between the company and their members.

"We have a group of ambassadors in our group, and they share honest reviews of our products and photos of them in use. Honesty is very important to us, and I always ask our ambassadors to share the pros and cons of every product they review for us. No product is perfect and I want any drawbacks highlighted. Customers trust us because of our complete honesty rather than just blank reviews that every product is 'amazing.'"

Wendy's three biggest community-building tips for existing brands:

- Promote your group to your customers so they are encouraged to join.
- Communicate and interact regularly with members.
- Encourage members to participate in discussions and share their lives.

Find out more about The Nappy Lady:

thenappylady.co.uk

@TheNappyLady

HIKE YOUR OWN HIKE

The last adventure I went on was called the Three Lakes Expedition. Over a cocktail in London, my friend Emma Rosen and I decided we were both in need of an adventure. We agreed that we wanted it to be something that hadn't been done before. Eventually, we settled on packrafting (lightweight inflatable rafts) and hiking between the longest, deepest, and highest lakes in England, which all sit in the Lake District. In between, we'd be wild camping and carrying all our own gear.

As with all my adventures, I shared our experience on my social media channels. When I returned from the five-day expedition, I was surprised that people's first reactions were just focusing on how hard it looked. It's true…it was very grueling. The bags were incredibly heavy, my body sore from the weight and walking for miles on end, I barely slept, unable to get comfortable on my roll mat, and the blisters on my hands from the long paddles…they hurt!

But the experience was so much more than that. It was beautiful views, a sense of being pioneers (no one has ever done this before), of heart-felt conversations with a good friend, moments where we laughed so hard I could barely breathe, quiet pauses paddling in the middle of a stunning lake, meeting interesting people, and a sense of achievement that's simply impossible to feel without all those struggles that got you there.

While everyone was focusing and just wanting to talk about the challenges, they missed what really mattered. Sure, it was hard, but it was so bloody brilliant as well!

You might have gotten to the end of this book and wondered, with all the challenges that come with building an online community, what is the point of it all? I worked my butt off for years free of charge, chipping away at my ambition. It was a constant uphill struggle. Then, when I finally felt like I was making serious progress—far from my problems being over—they only seemed to increase. I now had a group that took a huge amount of moderating, everyone buying for my time, and a team of volunteers and staff to now manage. The buck always stops with the community leader, all the problems falling in their lap. Just like me, if you take on this journey, you will make mistakes. When you do, everyone will know about it because that's just the nature of a community, and they will sting extra because this is your baby, your time, and your passion.

So yeah…it's not easy!

But just like an adventure, there's something incredible that comes with running a community. Something that only other community leaders will fully understand. You are the magician, the glue, the one who gets the satisfaction of going to bed each night knowing you're actually making a real, raw, honest difference in the world. That feeling—it's unbeatable!

It's a damn rollercoaster of a ride and you should be ready for it. On Wednesday night I was in tears when I received an angry email from a teammate wanting to leave out of the blue, feeling the brunt of my errors and her miscommunications. On Friday morning I was in tears because I had the pleasure of reading an email from a lady who had benefited from one of our community grants. In it she wrote:

"I didn't know what to expect from Love Her Wild, but nothing could have prepared me for what I experienced during that one weekend in May. I reconnected with nature, learnt new skills, and left empowered and inspired. Below the surface a fire was rekindled within me. It sounds cliche, but I feel I have found my tribe, a community that accepts me, women who will support me and a space where I no longer feel alone."

That email took my breath away. I made that happen! Words like that—they stay with you and heal the wounds. They make it all worth it.

At times you will feel fraught with the emotional turmoil of it all. This is why, above all else, you must prioritize self-care and compassion for yourself. Adopt healthy working habits from the start; move your body; rest your mind; build a support network around you that you can lean on in hard times; connect with others on social media who get it (you can always reach out to me @bex_band); know when you need a break; keep learning, growing, adapting, and changing; and never, *ever* beat yourself up for making mistakes.

The road ahead is long and bumpy, but you should be damn proud of taking the road less traveled.

Good luck.

Your tribe is waiting!

ACKNOWLEDGMENTS

You can't have a book about building online communities without first having one. So, my biggest thanks go to all the wonderful members, volunteers, staff, and supporters who make up the Love Her Wild community. I might be a little biased, but I think we're a pretty special bunch!

I'm hugely grateful to all the community leaders who kindly shared their stories and wisdom with me. And to Lucinda Literary and Post Hill Press for supporting me in getting this book onto the shelves of community leaders.

And finally, a special thanks to my husband Gil and his parents Amir and Mira who have always been my biggest believers when it came to launching my own business, chasing my ambitions, and making a success of being my own boss. I wouldn't be where I am today without you!

ABOUT THE AUTHOR

Author photo by Richard Tilney-Bassett

Bex Band is an adventurer and author. She founded one of the world's largest women's adventure communities, Love Her Wild. Her previous adventures include thru-hiking the 1,000 km Israel National Trail, kick-scooting the length of the USA, and kayaking the width of the UK against plastic pollution.

Bex has been recognized by *Business Leader* as the UK's top 30 inspiring entrepreneurs and was awarded the Next Generation Award by Enterprise Nation. For her work advocating for women in adventure, she has been shortlisted for a National Diversity Award, and in 2018 was given "Legacy Maker" status on the San Miguel "Alternative Rich List."

You can follow Bex on Facebook, Instagram, or Twitter (@ Bex_Band) or via her blog, which has had over a 1.5 million readers: www.bexband.com.

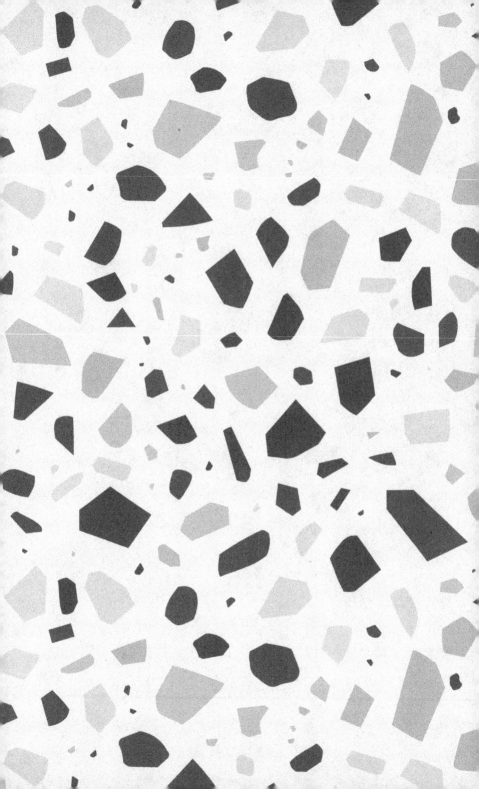

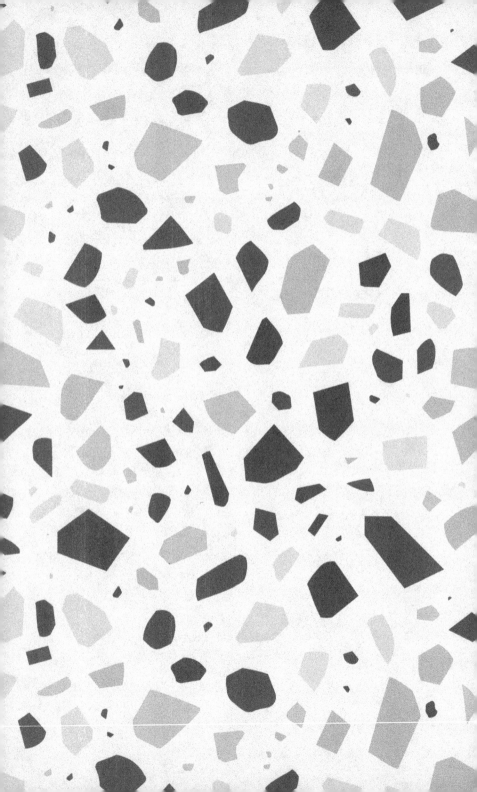